Praise

"A gripping geopo   rrent Russo-American lan   uow each ot

PETER WA   HOR, *FRONTIER* SERIES

"A fast-paced espionage thriller that reads like a movie. It will keep you in its grip to the very end."
GERARD LEE, AUTHOR, *TOP OF THE LAKE*

"A classic international thriller. Vivid characters and tight plotting make this a great read."
BRIAN STODDART, AUTHOR, *A HOUSE IN DAMASCUS*

"Jack Ryan meets Tucker Jones in the character of Neil Kyd in *Kyd's Game*, and by merging the plight of a father with the interests of governments, we get a story that balances fast-paced spy craft with the tenderness of a father's love for his daughter. I enjoyed every page of it."
READERS' FAVORITE

"With *Kyd's Game*, Rosenberg has created a story that is riveting, page-turning, and will keep readers on the edge of their seats until the shocking conclusion."
FEATHERED QUILL, BOOK REVIEWS

"*Kyd's Game* is teeming with unexpected twists and turns, making it an engaging read for all. Rosenberg's writing is masterful in its ability to maintain a sense of intrigue and suspense throughout the narrative."
THE US REVIEW OF BOOKS

About the Author

Marc Rosenberg grew up in Texas but has spent over half his adult life living and working as a screenwriter in Australia. At an early age he became an adventurer, taking a job as an estate agent in London, living for a year on a kibbutz and traveling overland through Asia.

Rosenberg has made films with Miles Davis, Daniel (Harry Potter) Radcliffe and Jeremy Irons, winning two Australian Writers' Guild Awards and the Los Angeles Fade-In Grand Prize for Best Original Screenplay. He has contributed to the journal *Film International*, written a book on screenwriting, *The Screenplay Tree*, and has taught extensively in the US, India, China and Australia.

An avid reader, he has a passion for espionage, crime and authentic character-based literature.

mrcrsnbrg.com

KYD'S GAME

MARC ROSENBERG

www.vineleavespress.com

Kyd's Game
Copyright © 2024 Marc Rosenberg

Cover design by Jessica Bell
Interior design by Amie McCracken

"Trust, but verify"
A Russian proverb

1

UNDER A COLD gunmetal sky, looking like a dull mirror, wind-swept and desolate, a small house and barn stood out against the flat white landscape. A single child's swing shivered in the frosty breeze. Wispy smoke swirling up from the chimney was the only sign of life until the clanking sound of metal on metal and a man's angry voice drew attention to a tractor and backhoe. "Fucking thing!" Unlike the tractor, Neil Kyd had no trouble admitting he was past his prime. He could hear himself sigh each time he sat down. Beard-stubbled, in a tattered army coat, gloves and stocking cap, ragged vapor chugged from his mouth. He'd had no intention of being stuck in Kansas, in winter, working on an unfixable tractor, but accepted this was where he needed to be. Two years earlier his eleven-year-old daughter had been diagnosed with Batten disease. It was a progressive and fatal nervous system disorder. Girls developed the symptoms later than boys but died sooner. As the disease slowly murdered Molly's body, her vision faded, her muscles cramped, and her breathing labored. There was nothing more he or the doctors could do. At best, she might struggle through another ten years of life. Kyd had left his job at the CIA in Langley, Virginia, and set up with Molly on his mother's farm. Kyd wasn't a farmer, that much he had no trouble proving.

Patty, his wife, had died of breast cancer when Molly was six, so she never had the heartache of seeing her daughter suffer.

Kyd's goal had been to finish excavation for a new septic tank, a task he had promised to complete during the summer when the ground was softer. He found prioritizing repairs around his mother's property had put him behind schedule, and of course the tractor was uncooperative. The hole was almost three yards deep and five feet wide with a large, galvanized water tank above. Coming to the conclusion that banging on the tractor's motor wasn't helping, Kyd put down his wrench, unscrewed the thermos sitting on the rusted front fender, and poured hot coffee into the plastic lid-cup. He could hardly feel the warmth through his gloves.

Above the rim of his cup, in the distance, he saw a black sedan approaching. There wasn't much doubt it was government issue, Kyd had used enough of them himself, nor did he suspect it had taken a wrong turn. He blew on his coffee and had time for a couple more sips before the car pulled up in front of the house.

The car's occupants had a brief discussion before Paul Wexler climbed out of the back seat. He was graying at the temples and there was luggage under the eyes. The driver stayed inside with the engine running. Hair freshly cut, Wexler was elegantly attired, wearing a black cashmere overcoat. Even though he'd worked at the Agency for thirty years, he was still eager to impress. Wexler surveyed the desolate white landscape above the roof of his car, even though he'd just spent the last hour driving through it. He put his collar up against the frigid breeze then looked toward Kyd and approached, quizzical smile on his face, icy snow crunching beneath his shiny black loafers. Where had he thought he was coming?

Wexler spoke Russian. "Kind of lonely out here, isn't it?" His breath came out in little clouds.

As far as Kyd could remember, these were the first words they'd exchanged in any language for over two years. Kyd replied in Russian. "You should see it off-season." His sense of humor, as his life, had become ironic.

Wexler stopped on the other side of the tractor, far enough away to avoid getting dirty, and switched to English. "Good to see you, Kyd." Only Kyd's mother used his first name.

"Even as head of Russia your accent sucks," Kyd said. His smile faded quickly, the rest of his face refusing to go along.

"You've kept track." It was hard to tell if Wexler was proud or defensive.

Kyd threw out what was left of his coffee and moved around the tractor to greet his guest. "Congratulations, Paul." The men shook gloved hands. It wasn't so much that Kyd disliked Wexler, liking had nothing to do with it. It was more that he never trusted him. This wasn't at all uncommon in a business where people were paid to keep secrets. Kyd had worked with him a few times, and there had been some friction, control issues, but the outcome was good and the Agency was pleased.

Wexler stomped his feet and blew into his cupped hands, even though he was wearing gloves. His ears had turned scarlet. "Can we go inside before I freeze my ass off?"

Kyd gained some sadistic pleasure out of taking his time. As they passed Wexler's car, Kyd bent down to look through the window and saw a woman, a young redhead, behind the wheel. "She okay in there?"

"That's Agent Barnes, she's got the heater full-blast," Wexler answered.

Agent Barnes gave Kyd a thumbs-up and Wexler followed Kyd to the house's front door, once more looking out at the desolate landscape. "What do you grow out here?"

"This is Kansas, they grow wheat." Kyd was careful not to say "we."

Everything inside the living room was old, except for Molly, covered in a blanket, sitting in the corner of a threadbare couch. Her curious, bright blue eyes were magnified behind thick glass lenses, made even brighter against a ghostly complexion. There was an oxygen tank beside her, and an open schoolbook on her lap. The TV was playing a teen soap, brats confessing infatuations and betrayals behind hallway locker doors. Kyd took off his hat and coat, hanging them on a peg at the entrance, leaving his boots underneath.

Wexler approached the couch. "You must be Molly. We met once when you were little."

Molly's speech was slurred, and Kyd needed to interpret what she was trying hard to say. "She wants to know if you knew her mother."

"Sure, I did. You look just like her." This pleased Molly. Patty had worked at the Agency briefly, where Kyd met her. Wexler asked her out once, but she was already dating Kyd. Patty later told him she thought Wexler was "sad." She was a kind person.

Margaret Kyd, rosy cheeks, thin as a broomstick, having detected an alien voice, rushed into the room from the kitchen as if she were late to her own party. Her baggy wool sweater, decorated with penguins, covered the top half of her apron. "Now, who's this handsome fellow?" Margaret demanded.

"This is Paul Wexler, a guy I used to work with." Kyd introduced him without enthusiasm.

"Neil, why don't you take Mr. Wexler's lovely coat?" She concentrated on Wexler while he removed his overcoat. "We promise to give it back," Margaret added. Beneath the coat was a tailored suit and tie. "Oh my, look at you." It was as if she'd discovered a unicorn in her closet.

"This is my mother, Margaret," Kyd explained.

"It's a pleasure." Wexler took a strategic step back, wary the old lady might lunge.

Kyd hung Wexler's coat, while Margaret, not taking the hint, invaded their guest's space. "May I offer you a cup of coffee, get you something to eat? I believe we still have some shortbread if Neil hasn't eaten it all."

Wexler took another step back. "No thank you, Margaret. Unfortunately, this has to be a quick visit," Wexler told her.

"I wouldn't mind a sandwich, if it's not too much trouble," Kyd ventured, but he couldn't be sure Margaret even heard, she was still admiring their guest. Kyd turned to Wexler and pointed down the hallway. "We can go down here." It went without saying that whatever it was that brought Wexler to the boondocks would need to be private. Kyd then turned to Molly, who had been watching the conversation as if she had a front row seat at the circus. "You finish your homework?"

Molly gathered herself to speak. "Almost."

"We'll drop it off after the hospital, okay?"

Molly nodded agreement, and Kyd led Wexler down the hall.

.

The office was small and square, with a window looking out onto Wexler's car, the exhaust blossoming. Kyd arranged himself in a battered, red vinyl armchair, gray duct tape mended the tears. He stretched out his legs, soaking up the warmth from a little electric heater glowing near his stockinged feet. With the door closed the room was almost comfortable. Wexler looked around the office. There was plenty to inspect—dusty old ledgers in a corner, some parts to equipment long since extinct, and shelves of books from a past life.

"You inherited this place from your father?" Wexler asked.

"It's Margaret's," Kyd corrected. His father had been far too practical to have ever entrusted Kyd with the farm, but as it turned out, he died before he could sell it. There was a picture on the wall of Kyd with Patty just out of the hospital, holding baby Molly. It hadn't been an easy birth, but Patty's smile broke through her exhaustion. She had loved being a mother. Beside it was a photo of Kyd, fifteen, with his dad, square jawed, crewcut, holding rifles, standing in front of an elk strapped to the hood of the car. His dad didn't mind showing off. It was the only time Kyd could remember when his father was less than disappointed in him. It was worth a photo. Kyd's rifle was mounted above the photo, gathering dust.

"Molly does look like Patty," Wexler said. He turned his attention to the collection of Russian literature squeezed onto shelves, running a finger across spines of books in Arabic, German and Spanish. Kyd believed if you wanted to under-stand a culture, language was the key, and he had an ear for it. Language got him out of Kansas. In an earlier life, before abusing tractors, he'd earned a PhD, teaching linguistics at Columbia University.

Wexler wasn't much interested in anything he looked at, he was working himself up to something. Kyd had to wait, remem-bering what it was like working with Wexler-types. They all felt undervalued, and habitually tried to leverage situations to their advantage. Manipulation was their occupation, a type of revenge. Kyd wouldn't give him the satisfaction of asking why he'd come, of showing interest. He'd have to tell Kyd without encouragement.

"Nicoli Petrov wants to be Russia's next president." Wexler glanced in Kyd's direction.

"Is that so?" Kyd knew this, anyone interested in Russia knew this, but maybe Wexler doubted Kansas had internet.

Wexler went on, "He's a human rights advocate and popular. It could be good for us." He pulled a copy of the Qur'an from Kyd's shelf and flipped through it as if he'd found an in-flight magazine.

"Because we're champions for human rights." His sarcasm wasn't lost on Wexler.

"Nicoli would also be more open-minded about our goals in the Middle East."

"If he got elected," Kyd pointed out.

"Garin likes being president." Garin had been Russia's president for seventeen years.

"I've heard that." Kyd's feet were getting hot, and he pulled them in.

Wexler put the Qur'an flat on the shelf, not where he'd found it. "But our Nicoli has an ace up his sleeve. He says he has graphic evidence the current president was complicit in attacking Syria with chemical weapons, probably sarin or a hyped-up derivative—men, women, children. Horrendous stuff." Wexler didn't seem horrified, it came across as if he were working out his tax return. "Even though the majority of Russians have no interest in Syria or Muslims, seeing children convulsing and hemorrhaging would get their sympathy. Nicoli believes, once seen, this would put him over the top." With his accounting over, he looked to Kyd for a reaction.

Kyd understood Petrov would never be allowed to screen anything antigovernmental in Russia. He'd end up in a Siberian work camp or be served a uranium cocktail. Kyd guessed the strategy was to broadcast the evidence in the West, knowing it would filter back. "Which brings you to Kansas," Kyd summed up, getting a hint for why Wexler had come.

"Nicoli has a camcorder video disk and wants to give it to you personally."

"Camcorder? I thought those were extinct."

"He's convinced you're the only one he can trust." Wexler sat on a straight-backed chair facing Kyd, the creases in his trousers still sharp. "It may have something to do with his sister. You were close friends, correct?" There was the trace of a smirk.

So, there it was, typical, a wild-assed scheme that took him forty minutes to unveil. Three years before he met Patty, Kyd was invited to Russia by an ex-student, Irina Petrov, Nicoli's younger sister. Nicoli had not yet appeared on the political radar and Kyd never met him. Kyd hadn't met much of anyone. There were many days and nights in Irina's small apartment when they never left her bedroom. Kyd knew Irina had fallen in love with him, she told him so, but after a year in Moscow, he couldn't imagine a future there or with Irina. It didn't feel right. He could see the writing on the wall. She was too young, and outside the bedroom, not that agreeable. Her naïve monopoly on The Truth lost its charm. It was a painful breakup Kyd wished he'd handled better. Irina refused to stay in contact. Kyd wasn't surprised that Wexler had this information, or that he'd try to use it, but he was surprised Irina had recommended him.

"Why can't they send it digitally, isn't that how things get done these days, encrypted and all that?"

"The original would need to be verified and he's worried about security. A couple of our couriers had problems even delivering Irina's message." "Problems" came across as insufficient postage.

"Are you asking me to go get it, Paul?" Kyd felt sure once it was said out loud, Wexler would see how ridiculous his request was. Perhaps he'd been asked to give it the good ole college try, knowing if Kyd refused, they'd shift to a plan B.

But no, Wexler was unstoppable. "It's all set up. You'd have our full support. Once you bring it back, we'll examine it, and if it's the real deal, make it public and see what happens. The election's getting close, everything needs to move quickly."

Kyd listened with a reluctant appreciation for Wexler's salesmanship. He was smart not to bring patriotism into it, they'd both been in government too long for that. "Can't. Won't. First, you don't know for sure what's on this video disk. It could be something a desperate politician cooked up. It's happened before. Second, will it change the election results? No one knows. It's a Hail Mary at best. But above everything else, I won't leave Molly."

"Petrov is adamant it has to be you," Wexler restated.

Kyd stood up, signaling the end of the conversation. "Not going to happen, Paul. Sorry you wasted your trip."

Wexler stayed seated. "What if we were to offer you a quid pro quo? You do this for us, and we can do something for you."

Kyd didn't need a refresher course in Latin. "What, will the Agency fix our tractor?" He could see the prehistoric machine through the window, still grumpy.

"If that's what it takes."

"We're done, Paul."

Wexler wasn't moving. He took in a lung full of air, sighing deeply. "You must have noticed Molly's disease is progressing more aggressively than predicted, or anyone had hoped," he said, shaking his head with concern. "She's in pretty bad shape."

Since when had he become so concerned about his daughter's health? Kyd stared at Wexler and didn't see sympathy, only calculation. "You just walked in. What are you talking about?" Kyd tried to keep the anger out of his voice.

It was as if Wexler were delivering a eulogy. "I'm sorry, but I don't think your doctors are being completely honest, or maybe they're just overly optimistic. Molly's recent test results show early onset dementia, and her lung capacity has quickly deteriorated from 32 to 27 percent. If not already, she'll be experiencing violent and uncontrollable seizures." Wexler hesitated and waited to catch Kyd's eyes. "At her current rate of decline she might not last the year."

Kyd's fists were clinched, it was as if Wexler were spying through a keyhole. "You've been in her medical records?"

"You could ask to see the file yourself, it's all there." Wexler intertwined his fingers, resting them on his crossed legs, the sad uncle.

Was it true? Kyd hadn't noticed any major decline. Some days weren't as good as others, but he hadn't seen her records, he'd trusted the doctors.

Wexler then said what he was prepared to say all along. "There are trials being conducted on Batten using embryonic stem cell therapy. Cutting edge stuff. The results are very positive. The trials are strictly limited, long waiting list and very expensive." He aimed to use Molly as a political pawn. Kyd was close enough that Wexler had to look up at him. Kyd needed to keep his hands in his pockets. If Wexler was aware of the danger, he didn't show it. "What if we see to it Molly is accepted into the program and the costs are covered?"

Kyd knew about the therapy and had applied, but with the waiting list, Molly would be well beyond help before she received treatment, even if he could afford it.

"It would be a win-win," Wexler assured Kyd.

Kyd knew whatever they proposed would have sharp edges, but he was teased by hope. He turned to the window, Agent Barnes' hazy silhouette was just visible inside the car. He couldn't imagine what she would be doing in there. Listening to music? What kind? "This is something you would guarantee, regardless of the outcome?" Kyd's words bounced back at him off the fogged glass.

"As long as you make a genuine effort." Wexler talked to Kyd's back. "In and out, a couple of days, tops." There was a long pause, and Wexler felt Kyd needed to be nudged. "They'll only give it to you."

Kyd heard the legs of Wexler's chair scrape the floor. "I've been out of the game a long time," Kyd reminded him.

"Like riding a bike." Wexler opened the door to leave. "Don't take too long to decide. I need your answer by tomorrow."

Kyd didn't turn around, didn't shake hands. He heard muffled goodbyes and watched through the window as Wexler climbed into his car. "Win-win." That's what he said.

"He dresses nicely." Margaret had come in, holding out a plate with a sandwich.

"Yes, he does."

·

In the pickup, Molly sat squeezed between Margaret and Kyd, Kyd driving. He'd shaved and was wearing fresh clothes. It had begun to snow again, and Wexler's tire tracks had almost disappeared. Molly was breathing heavily, leaning on her grandmother's shoulder.

"You okay, sweetie?" Margaret asked, and Molly nodded.

Kyd couldn't imagine how Molly saw the state of her condition, or if she could even remember when she was well. They hadn't told her too much about her fate because knowing wouldn't do her any good. Her disloyal body would let her know. Kyd cleared his throat before beginning. "If I needed to go away for a few days, any chance you girls could manage on your own?"

Margaret looked over at him, surprised. "Where're you going?"

"I'll be back in a week." His eyes were focused on the road ahead, not wanting to see his mother's reaction.

Margaret accepted he wasn't going to answer her question. "I guess we could manage, couldn't we Mol?" She caressed Molly's head. "He can't even fix our tractor."

Sitting up, Molly swallowed a breath. "Because of Mr. Wexler?"

Kyd turned to her. "He thinks he can help us."

Molly focused her bright eyes on her father. "You have to do something first …"

He was reminded of how good she was at connecting dots. This short phrase exhausted her lungs and she gasped for air.

Margaret held the oxygen mask over her face. "Put your head back. Try to relax." Margaret looked at Kyd. "Maybe you should drive faster."

Kyd accelerated.

Kyd parked outside the emergency entrance, carrying Molly into the hospital—she was a feather. Margaret had called ahead, and the doctors were waiting. As they put Molly onto a gurney, the muscles in her back tightened like an archer's bow, making her an unwilling contortionist. Her body went into violent spasms.

Outside the emergency room, Kyd could see his daughter's eyes roll back and her teeth clench. Margaret held Molly's hand, as nurses in green scrubs circled her bed like bees around a hive.

Kyd used his cell phone to tell Wexler what he wanted to hear.

2

IT WAS 10:00 a.m. before all fifteen members of the UN Security Council were finally seated. The rounded horseshoe of desks made it easier for members to view their fellow representatives across the chamber. Nameplates in front of each ambassador identified their home country. Close to a hundred aides and councilors scurried behind the ambassadors, making notes and delivering documents they might need. The US ambassador, a jowly woman in her late fifties with gray hair, was recognized by the council president. The chamber became quiet.

She pulled the microphone close and spoke with solemn intent, her words translated through headphones for anyone not fluent in English. "Mr. President, fellow members, ladies and gentlemen, we do not need to be reminded of what chemical weapons can do, the horrific effects." She looked around the room, her voice steady. "I have recently received credible reports that the Syrian government is using the chemical agent sarin to attack opposition forces. This is an abhorrent and clear violation of international law." The ambassador then fixed her gaze on her male, Russian counterpart sitting opposite, also in his fifties and gray. He returned her calculated gaze, as two pugilists might before a heavyweight fight. "We will soon have evidence that the Russian government has been complicit in

22

these attacks." The Russian shook his head in disgust, a dismissive smile on his lips. He was prepared to counterpunch. She continued, "The United States appeals to the Syrian president and the Russians to cease the use of chemical weapons immediately and to be held accountable." The quiet chamber stirred, and her microphone crackled as she yielded the floor.

The Russian ambassador, seemingly appalled by the accusation, was recognized.

CIA Deputy Director Clyde Sorrow, late forties, suit and tie, sat behind his desk watching the Russian's aggrieved rebuttal on his computer screen. Behind him was a portrait of the US president. "These charges are reprehensible. The Russian Federation categorically denies these unfounded accusations." Sorrow could practically see the indignant spittle bursting from the ambassador's lips. "We, like the rest of the world, see the use of chemical weapons as a dangerous and monstrous crime." He surveyed the room, recognizing allies. "As seems routine now, the United States willingly throws around accusations based on nothing other than its need to distract this chamber from its own military support for terrorists in the Syrian Arab Republic." He paused for dramatic effect. "If chemical weapons have been used in any form, we have no knowledge of it." The Russian ambassador found the American ambassador's eyes. "Let us see your proof."

Sorrow smiled.

3

Looking out from the third-floor balcony, Major Alexi Zarefsky could see Russia's first McDonald's. It was on the other side of Pushkin Square, still the largest in Europe, he'd been told. Muscovites refused to believe they weren't part of Europe, even though the rest of the world was taught Asia began at Istanbul, Turkey. Who was to say? Who made the rules?

Down below, between Zarefsky and the Golden Arches, nearly eight thousand stalwarts gathered, braving the freezing cold weather. They were promised a hero and chanted, "Nicoli ... Nicoli ... Nicoli ..." Occasionally there would be a lull, then the chant would pick up again, rolling through the crowd like a set of sonic waves. It was past 3:00 p.m., some supporters having arrived before dawn. They wanted to get as close to the speaker's platform as possible. The crowd surged, fed from side streets, arteries pushing blood to the heart. Volunteer militia, easily identified by orange and black St. George ribbons, worked their way into the crush, while *kosmonauts*, riot police wearing their trademark bulbous helmets and carrying assault rifles, surrounded the periphery.

The incumbent president, Maksim Garin, had reigned for almost two decades, and was not terribly upset to be called "the new czar." Garin had never been accused of tolerance, and it was widely accepted he used the persuasive arguments he'd learned from his time in the KGB to eliminate opposition. Whether this persuasion took the form of extortion, blackmail or mysterious disappearances, dissent was discouraged. It was also an open secret that Garin's loyal ministers, despite their meager government salaries, owned mansions on the Volga River and made regular shopping expeditions to Paris or New York. Corruption was a common topic of conversation in private, but apart from a few "radicals," was accepted as a necessary evil. Discussions would begin with "Can you believe ...?" and end with a shrug of the shoulders and "What can be done?" Then, deciding it was his time, Nicoli Petrov threatened to overturn this perception. He was a dashing, intelligent and morally conscious candidate, Russia's answer to John F. Kennedy. He talked about ending corruption and openly accused Garin of criminal activity, something no previous candidate was foolish enough to do. The government's covert, clumsy and contradictory smear campaign, claiming Petrov was either a homosexual or whoremonger, hadn't dented his popularity; in fact, it seemed to improve his chances.

Major Zarefsky had been summoned by the minister of internal affairs. He'd been waiting on the office balcony for an hour to find out why. As far as Zarefsky knew, he hadn't said or done anything out of line, and it was unlikely someone of the minister's standing would bend low enough to deal with minor infractions. He waited for his answer. At first glance, Zarefsky appeared thuggish, his bull-like body stuffed into a police uniform, but once he moved, that impression disappeared. There was an unhurried, thoughtful economy in his actions, without patience for distraction or uncertainty. His colleagues and subordinates had a respectful unease around him, something he recognized and found useful. Major Zarefsky wasn't a member of the normal *politsiya*, he had risen through the ranks as an officer in OMOH, the special purpose police unit, an internal security force.

"We've met before, I believe." Minister Bortnik had pushed out of the thick glass doors and joined Zarefsky at the railing. The major's back stiffened as if he were on review. Bortnik was part of the president's inner circle, having followed Garin from the KGB. In his late sixties, he was thin and stooped, with cloudy sunken eyes. The minister looked Zarefsky over, adjusting in his mind the assessment he'd received.

"Yes, sir, once before. I was part of an army delegation." Zarefsky couldn't help but be flattered that someone thought he was important enough to research. The major had been one of twenty officers that had gathered in Bortnik's office ten years earlier. They received medals after the Second Chechen War. The puckered scars from bullet wounds in his thigh and shoulder told more than any medal.

Bortnik extended his gloved hand and Zarefsky shook it. "Thank you for coming on such short notice, Major. I hope it didn't cause too much inconvenience."

There were no longer inconveniences when it came to work. Zarefsky was living on his own, his marriage having ended three months before, only papers to be signed. Sofia, after fifteen years, had told him out of the blue that she was "unhappy," and there was nothing he could do about it. She assured him she wasn't having an affair. The reason was a growing numbness in their relationship that suffocated her joy. *Her joy.* She hadn't blamed him with words, but he felt her restrained anger. He saw no point in arguing, he couldn't be sure what he'd be arguing about. People felt the way they felt, it was only their behavior that could be questioned. He and Sofia didn't have children, so parting was clinical. He moved into a small apartment closer to the city, a short train ride to where he stood.

"I'm at your service, sir," Zarefsky assured the minister.

The excitement below had grown, and now there was cheering. Both men looked down to the Square, as the crowd pushed forward. Wedged between two burly guards, a woman made her way on stage. She wore a fur hat, the wind making fluttering wings of her raven hair. Despite her intention to be a person of the people, Irina Petrov appeared regal, it came naturally to her. Her guards stayed behind as she strode toward the microphone, tapping it with a manicured fingernail. It crackled to life as the crowd bounced on tiptoe, looking over the heads of those in front. She gazed out at the sea of hopeful, chilled faces swaying as a wave. "Good afternoon, I am the sister of your next president ..." Saying the words, the recognition of where she was, what she was doing, seemed to suddenly catch her by surprise.

The crowd erupted in cheers. "Nicoli ... Nicoli ... Nicoli ..."

Irina joined them for a moment with a nervous grin, caught up in the swelling energy, then raised a hand and waited until the chanting had died down. "It is one thing to wish for a just society, but quite another to risk your life for one. In this respect, we have no more courageous advocate than my brother, Nicoli Petrov!"

The cheers became deafening, as a slim man in his early fifties approached behind Irina. Nicoli looked like a library academic, with shaggy graying hair and wire-rimmed glasses. His posture and stride projected a defiant confidence, as if fighting a strong headwind. He and Irina exchanged kisses and a hug before he held up a hand to quieten the crowd. "Thank you, my friends.

Thank you, my friends and fellow patriots." His voice resonated with youthful vitality.

On an adjacent balcony, a voluptuous, fur-coated, and rosy-cheeked woman was caught up in the excitement. She turned, recognized the minister, and waved. He nodded in her direction, and for a moment, the weight of years lifted.

"You see, this is why it is important to be nice to your sister." Petrov gripped Irina's waist in a one-armed hug, before she stepped back, making him the center of attention.

The minister continued to appraise the friendly woman on the next balcony but spoke to Zarefsky. "Democracy is very stimulating, don't you agree, Major?"

"As you say, Minister," Zarefsky replied.

Bortnik turned to Zarefsky. "But as we have found out with any stimulant, there can be negative side effects."

The major was unsure if the minister was soliciting his agreement, but he didn't have time to make that decision. Bortnik gestured toward Petrov below. "Our charming 'Nic-o-li' is a negative side effect. He's a traitor to Mother Russia." There was gravity in his voice but no alarm.

Zarefsky tuned out Petrov's speech and the crowd's cheering. He wasn't naïve; he knew that the president was threatened by Petrov's popularity but accusing him of treason was unexpected. Treason was a capital crime, punishable by death.

"Our intelligence sources tell us he will attempt to give classified information to an American spy. Information that would compromise our freely elected government." Bortnik captured the major's eyes. "The president would like you to recover this material."

If Zarefsky hadn't misheard, President Garin knew his name. This was an honor in itself.

Petrov's voice broke through. "We are at a crucial turning point in our country's history, a time when our leaders must put personal interests aside for the benefit of all Russians." There was wild applause.

The minister studied Zarefsky's face, attempting to see beneath the surface. "I recommended you because of your record. You are a dependable leader who can follow orders."

"Thank you, Minister." Zarefsky could think of nothing to add, he had the trust of the president. If the mission went well and he advanced, perhaps Sofia, another traitor, could find her joy with him again.

"It is important that neither Petrov nor the American spy escapes. They must answer for their crimes."

There was nothing to understand, these were orders.

Petrov's voice broke in. "We are a peaceful people, but even patience has its limits. It is time for change!"

"Change ... Change ... Change ..." The volume increased with each repetition, and the demand echoed off buildings around the Square.

The minister raised his voice to be heard. "Zarefsky isn't a Muslim name."

Zarefsky was caught off-guard. "My mother is Muslim." He hadn't tried to hide his heritage, but he didn't think it was relevant either. He had fought for the government against Muslim separatists. His loyalty couldn't be questioned.

A smile played on Bortnik's lips. "Good, you have deceit in your blood."

How was he deceitful, or how might deceit be expected? Zarefsky wiped that thought away, he would prove they had made the right choice. Everything else was irrelevant.

"Instructions are waiting for you. Keep me informed." Without more to say, the minister returned inside, leaving Zarefsky alone at the railing.

Nicoli Petrov's threat, now with more weight, reached the balcony. "Soon, I will expose the current government for the corrupt, immoral, and heartless regime it is. Russia deserves better, you deserve better ..." Petrov's words faded and Zarefsky stopped listening. The president knew his name.

4

THE FLIGHT FROM Kansas City to Sheremetyevo International Airport took almost twenty-four hours. Kyd's phone told him he'd landed at "19:53." The trip included a three-hour layover in New York and an aerial view of Greenland, which didn't look any colder than Kansas. Kyd, now "Douglas Reynolds," waited his turn in front of a windowed customs barricade. The agent's windows reflected the jet-lagged zombies standing around him, eager to reach their beds. Kyd did his best to avoid making eye contact with roaming immigration officers. He'd been taught looking in their direction created suspicion, something they were taught. Kyd reminded himself it would be the little things that would keep him safe. Having spoken to a few veteran operatives when he worked at the Agency, they stressed this. When eating, switching a fork from the left to the right hand gave you away as American. Nothing he had to worry about.

Agent Barnes had met him in the departure lounge at LaGuardia, his New York stopover. Kyd joked to himself that with a first name like "Agent," her career path would be limited to insurance or espionage. He didn't recognize her immediately. She was taller than he expected, he'd only seen her seated through a foggy car window. She wore soundless sneakers and might have passed for an Ivy League coed, red hair bouncing off her shoulders. Sitting together in a secluded corner, she unpacked a bulky office folder along with his new name. Because of his previous CIA affiliation and history with Irina, it made sense that using his real name would be counterproductive. Agent Barnes handed him a counterfeit passport, slightly worn with customs stamps from Turkey, Mexico, and Panama. He also received a driver's license and a couple of utility bills, all with his new name. Perhaps with Wexler's sense of humor, if he had one, Douglas Reynolds sold farm equipment, tractors. Kyd was also given several brochures and a diary to back it up. There hadn't been much imagination put into his new home address, he still lived in Kansas. Kyd supposed this was a defense against being quizzed on the state bird or flower, neither of which he knew. While his indoctrination seemed a little ad hoc, Kyd figured the arrangements and the documents would have taken time to prepare, maybe days before Wexler's visit. There had never been any doubt he would accept their deal—the quid pro quo. Agent Barnes, in her clipped, self-assured way, told Kyd everything had been scrupulously worked out and it would be a quick and simple roundtrip. Her smile was manufactured in a government factory—CIA Barbie. She waited for him to smile back, code to let her know he agreed with her care-free prediction. Kyd put his faith in knowing the Agency wanted Petrov's video disk badly enough to get him home again. The disk would be his life insurance policy, not the smile. Agent Barnes' confident optimism not matched, she left him with, "Good luck," which he thought was better than "break a leg." Too late, he did twist a smile, recalling the old blues refrain, "If it weren't for bad luck, I wouldn't have no luck at all."

Kyd didn't recognize the airport he'd been in twenty years before, the one with chipped linoleum floors and dirty windows. It was a cookie-cutter replica of every other international airport from LAX to SYD. Chrome and glass, with the ambush of duty-free goods most locals couldn't afford.

A young, fresh-faced female officer, behind her glass shield, raised her head as he arrived at her window. Her crisp, emerald-green uniform and tie was a punch in the weary eye. Seeing his passport, she practiced her English. "What is purpose of stay, Mister Rey-nolds?" He'd have to get used to his new name. She slid his passport through a scanning machine.

"I sell farm equipment. I have a meeting with Uralvagon-zavod." Kyd was careful to stumble through the name, in keeping with his non-Russian-speaking disguise. He was told they were one of the largest tractor manufacturers in Russia and his contact information, if they investigated, would check out.

She didn't seem to be listening, a concerned look on her face caused her eyebrows to knit. She scanned his passport again.

Kyd felt a thin sheen of perspiration arrive on his forehead. "Is there a problem?" Maybe Agent Barnes was right, this would be a quick trip.

Her eyebrows parted, returning home. "My machine is slow only." She returned his passport. "Have successful visit."

A male officer, whose eyes he avoided, waved Kyd past and signaled for the next person in line to step forward. With only a leather carry-on, he weaved his way through the bedraggled passengers waiting at the baggage carrousel and exited the Nothing to Declare door without incident.

Out of the hundred enthusiastic relatives, friends, and corporate chauffeurs, who looked Kyd over with disappointment, he saw a scruffy man in his thirties. He held a sign reading *Dogless Raynold*. His clothes looked too big for him, and he had a cigarette smoldering between his nicotine-stained fingers. If he was in disguise, it was a good one. Even though Kyd approached his driver directly, the man seemed blindsided.

Kyd continued with English. "Let's go."

"Dogless?" The driver wanted to make sure.

"Douglas. Yeh, let's go." Whatever was going to happen was going to happen, it was the fatalistic philosophy he'd adopted over the last few years—you do what you can, then stop worrying. He remembered Wexler's provision, "genuine effort," and that's all he intended to do.

"My name is Boris Khrushchev, easy for remembering," he volunteered. His yellowed teeth were visible behind an untrimmed moustache, death row inmates peering through rusty bars.

Boris reached out to take Kyd's bag, but Kyd pulled it away. "I've got it."

They headed toward the exit, Boris walking beside Kyd. "First time to Russia?"

"Boris, just take me where I need to go." He wasn't looking for friends or interested in a tour.

"Yes of course, what you say. Follow me."

Kyd couldn't be sure how much Boris knew about the purpose of his trip, but he knew enough to be nervous, twitchy. He lit another cigarette.

Inside Boris' car was a hanging forest of green air fresheners, and although it was freezing outside, in a considerate attempt to thin the constant stream of cigarette smoke, he'd opened his window. Kyd sat in the back, coat buttoned to the top, taking in the city. Like the airport, it had evolved. There were ten times the number of cars he remembered, and not just Zhigulis. There were parking meters, shopping malls, neon, buildings that looked like glass prisms and Starbucks—everywhere. Kyd tried to get his bearings, searching for landmarks, but couldn't see any—he could be in any modern city. It was impossible for him to separate his memories of Moscow from his memories of Irina, and how different his life would have been had he stayed. No Patty, no Molly. He could have traded his problems. Back then he thought of Russia as a straitjacket with Irina buckling the straps. Maybe it was the cultural divide. While Americans were renowned for their puppy-dog enthusiasm, Russians saw cheerfulness as a form of mental illness. Still, if Irina had recommended him for this job, maybe she'd forgiven him for leaving.

"You are here at exciting time, Mister Ray-nold." Boris wouldn't give up.

Kyd decided to be more polite, "hands across the water" and all that. "Is that so?" He pulled out his cell phone, the one Agent Barnes had given him.

"Yes, very so. We are on edge of revolution."

Kyd was punching in numbers. "Another one?"

Boris laughed, not immune to history. "Yes, but this one is better. Nicoli Petrov will bring true democracy."

Kyd spoke into his cell. "It's me … I'm fine. How's Molly?" He saw Boris' eyes in the rear-view mirror.

Margaret was standing beside Molly's hospital bed, cell phone to her ear. The room looked new, befitting a well-funded avant-garde treatment center. Molly sat up, breathing through an oxygen mask, IV in her arm. "Paul organized everything. He moved us to the clinic, and they started doing tests this morning. Everyone is very nice." Molly reached for the phone. "Molly wants to say something."

Molly lowered her oxygen mask so she could speak. Her voice was clear. "Where are you?" She listened. "Is it cold? ... Okay, everyone is friendly ... Don't worry ..."

As Kyd came to understand it, Batten disease was caused when the enzymes meant to break down and dispose of a cell's waste, weren't doing their job. As the garbage built up, the cells and eventually the victim died. In the operation Molly would undergo, a surgeon would inject stem cells from an embryo into her brain. New enzymes would replace the lazy ones. The hope was that the new stem cells would stop the deterioration even if they couldn't reverse it. Kyd took no comfort in knowing the disease was genetic, he and Patty both contributing to their daughter's painful suffering. Of course, Patty bailed with a clear conscience.

Kyd gazed out the window, but in his mind's eye he could see his daughter lying in her hospital bed attached to tubes, like a string puppet. "I'll be back before you know it," he said into the phone. This was the plan. Kyd wanted to be at her side before the actual treatments started. "I love you, sweetie ..." He listened to her response and hung up, putting the phone back in his pocket.

Boris was smiling in the mirror. "I have family. Two boys, crazy wife." He exposed his jaundiced teeth, speaking one father to another. Boris held up a photo on his dashboard so Kyd could see, guiding the car with the fingers holding the cigarette. In the photo Boris was the only one looking happy.

Boris' phone rang and he answered in Russian. "I'm dropping him off now." He hung up, and fighting two lanes of traffic, double-parked outside Arbatskaya Metro Station, the entrance resembling a Soviet star. Angry drivers in the cars behind, sat on their horns. "Here," Boris said.

Kyd surveyed the bustling station and the rugged-up business commuters pouring out. "Where do I go? Who am I meeting?"

Boris turned in his seat to face Kyd, the horns behind them getting angrier. "You take number-four train, blue, to Shchy-olkovskaya Station." He said the name again, pronouncing every syllable clearly. "Someone will meet you. Like clockwork." Boris was as satisfied as if he'd designed the plan himself.

"Someone will meet my train?" Kyd wanted to make sure he understood correctly.

"Like clockwork. No need worry," Boris assured him, lighting another cigarette.

Kyd looked at him a moment longer, seeing his driver had exhausted the information he'd been given. He opened his door and offered Boris a twenty-dollar bill. "Take your family to dinner." He wasn't sure how much anything cost.

Without much deliberation, Boris accepted the cash. "*Ochen khorosho, spasibo.*" Then realizing he'd spoken Russian, he translated. "Means very nice, thank you."

"I'll try to remember." Kyd grabbed his bag off the seat as the horns continued to blast.

Boris was unbothered, used to the furious chorus, pushing a business card in Kyd's direction. "I can show you Moscow."

Kyd moved past the card. "I won't be here that long."

"Keep, I have many. Very good rates."

Drivers were getting out of their cars, screaming abuse. Kyd took the card, putting it in his shirt pocket. Once the door was closed, Boris blasted his horn twice and wedged his way back into the traffic.

Inside the station, it was much as Kyd remembered, with a few electronic barnacles—self-serve ticket machines instead of windows with tellers, digital billboards instead of printed timetables and security cameras hanging from the ceiling like octopi eyes. Bored metro guards stood in corners smoking, kibitzing, and checking their cell phones. Muscovites had every reason to be proud of their underground system, there were 215 stops on fourteen lines. Metro passageways were decorated with polished red marble, chandeliers hung from ornate vaulted ceilings, and murals depicted battles, or significant Russian figures, each station offering a different cultural appreciation lesson.

Kyd inserted fifty-five rubles into a red electronic kiosk, part of his CIA allowance, and the machine spat out a ticket. Checking out the billboard displaying stations and departure times in colorful animation, he was aware of being watched. It felt like a thin draft on the back of his neck, but looking for an observer was useless. Several passengers returned his gaze, rightly sensing he didn't belong.

5

NICOLI PETROV SAT at a small round library table on the second floor of the CPA, Moscow's Central Party Archive, next to the open atrium, a newspaper spread out in front of him. Dressed in dark green corduroy jacket and tie, he waited to meet Irina's contact. Nicoli was impatient by nature and fidgeted. He enjoyed the solitude of the Archive, there was less and less as his popularity grew.

"He's on his way." The voice was deep and resonant.

Nicoli walked to the iron filigreed railing and saw his bodyguard looking up at him from the ground floor. The guard waited for acknowledgement.

"Thank you, Joseph." He checked his watch; it was 10:20. The guard disappeared into an adjoining storage room. Nicoli looked at his fingertips and when he saw they were darkened by newsprint wiped them clean on his pants, sat, and checked his watch again.

Nicoli and Irina, four years younger, had not been close. She had traveled to America for graduate studies, while Nicoli continued his social activism in Moscow. It wasn't until a reckless, drunken driver killed their father crossing the road, that the siblings were drawn together. They came to recognize each other's value. Irina was practical, attractive, while Nicoli was introverted, the passionate idealist. During their father's wake, lubricated by a few vodkas, he told Irina he wanted to create a new Russia, to work against the endemic corruption and waste. She didn't laugh; she developed a plan.

Information about the camcorder recording came as a surprise, not because Nicoli believed the government was incapable of heinous acts, but that graphic evidence existed. He knew the general election would be rigged and he could never win by just a little. Proof the Russian government participated in chemical attacks on defenseless civilians might be just enough to put him over the threshold. If nothing else, it would shine an international light on President Garin's dark soul.

The next step had to be making the evidence public. Irina told Nicoli she had met Kyd when he was a professor at Columbia University, and he had a connection to the Central Intelligence Agency. She trusted him, and Nicoli suspected there was more she didn't say, but whatever his doubts, he realized his options were limited. They were running out of time.

A movement across the atrium caused Petrov to look up, he knew rats also found the Archive accommodating.

6

KYD RODE THE escalator down to the number-four train platform, a few stories below. After 10:00 p.m., the number of commuters thinned, but there were still enough to break a fall. Once when he was descending in the early hours, he had seen a young drunken woman in stilettos tumble halfway down. Blood streaming down her head, she righted herself, and, grinning, staggered away.

Kyd turned, looking for someone who might be following, unsure how this "clockwork" operation would play out. He understood a wink, a nod or subtle gesture might be a tell. If he was given the video disk in an hour or two he'd be home before Molly's treatments began. This was the plan.

Three boisterous teenagers, laughing and shouting, ran past him, rocking an old woman a step ahead. Kyd was just able to grab her elbow before she fell.

She screamed after them, "Thugs!" They didn't hear or pretended not to, halfway down. Commuters close by shrugged their shoulders as if to say "What else can one expect?" Kyd let go of her arm when she regained her footing. The old woman seemed like the eccentric, wrinkled old aunt you only saw at Christmas and funerals, the one with a house full of cats. She spoke loudly to compensate for a loss of hearing. "This Russia now, foreigners and criminals!" She tried to look back at Kyd without losing her balance.

They reached the platform just as the train arrived, entering after passengers got off. Kyd found an empty bench seat facing the direction of travel. The old woman had choices but sat beside him, as if he'd become her personal savior. She appraised Kyd, noticing his travel bag. Her glasses were smudged with grimy fingerprints. "You're on holiday?" she wanted to know.

"Visiting a friend," he replied in Russian.

"Ah, friends, all dead. Eh?" She waited for an answer and Kyd nodded. He wondered how many trains she rode a day, looking for people she could talk to. He was lucky with Margaret.

The carriage had filled, and a Muslim woman wearing a dirty hooded parka over her burka sat opposite. The old woman zeroed in on her, unwilling to move her knobby knees out of the way. The old woman's contempt was bright, she spoke loud enough for the Muslim passenger to hear. "They cover their faces because they're thieves. Moscow is no longer Moscow. Arabs, Turks, Indians—we're outsiders in our own country. This is democracy!" She spat the words, staring at the Muslim sitting across the narrow aisle. The old woman turned to Kyd for support.

The Muslim stared back at them and hissed in Arabic, "Kiss my ass."

Kyd hid a smile while the women continued to stare at one another.

"Can't even speak Russian." The old woman turned back to Kyd. "Part of a tribe. A tribe of terrorists."

As the train pulled into the next station, the old woman wobbled to her feet, Kyd's hand preventing her from falling backward. "Thank you, sir. A true Russian gentleman. Have a safe holiday." She staggered to the sliding doors and stepped off.

The Muslim woman stared at Kyd, stinging him with her eyes. He turned away, looking out the train's dark window. Kyd saw his ghostly reflection and accepted it was a true picture of how he felt. The window also mirrored the Muslim woman taking the seat beside him, traveling in the same direction.

"Next stop," she spoke in English.

Kyd turned, surprised but uncertain. "Irina?" He couldn't be sure; it had been too long since he'd heard her voice.

She stood and moved toward the door. Kyd followed.

The station was busy, near three universities. Elektrozavodskaya Station was named after a nearby light bulb factory. The ceiling above the platform was decorated with over 300 globes. Kyd followed his guide, climbing the escalator, maneuvering between other passengers, neither of them speaking. He had trouble keeping up with her. No one would guess they were together, which he supposed was the whole point. Then reaching the top, she slipped through the metro crowd like a sleek eel. Kyd stopped, craning his neck, hoping to see her waiting, or thinking if he stood still she might double back. She didn't. After a minute of being buffeted by commuters, he moved to the exit. "Genuine effort," he reminded himself.

It was snowing more heavily and a stiff breeze pushed the white flakes sideways. Kyd pulled his collar up, taking a step back, out of the wind. He looked in all directions, but the woman he thought was Irina had disappeared. It could be she saw something she didn't like, or got cold feet, it was the weather for it. He agreed with himself he'd wait ten more minutes then head for the airport. This plan cheered him, the whole operation seemed improbable from the beginning. The idea a video disk, no matter how explicit, could change the results of a Russian election was a romantic dream. Kyd checked his watch again.

"This way." Irina was behind him. Without waiting, she walked ahead at a brisk pace. "You had no problems?" There wasn't a lot of concern, more a way of reassuring herself he was behind her.

"No problems." He hoped for a flicker of warmth. After all, hadn't she asked for his help?

They turned a corner and approached a dirty gray sedan. Irina unlocked the car and slid behind the wheel. Kyd walked around and entered the opposite side, grateful to escape the sharp gusty breeze.

Once she had the engine going, she adjusted the heater. Twisting out of her coat and removing her burka, she settled. He had his first look at Irina's face. A strong mature beauty had replaced a younger woman's playful innocence. There were a few fine lines around her eyes but no trace of gray hair. She was more attractive than in the photos he'd found on the internet.

Irina could feel him looking at her and turned to face him. "So, you're here," she said finally.

"I'm here." The confirmation helped anchor him.

She pulled away from the curb, into the sparse traffic. The snow was building and he could hear the heavy flakes hit the windshield like little punches. Irina put her wipers on. A moment of silence passed. As questions swirled around in Kyd's head, he couldn't be sure any would be welcome.

"Nicoli looks forward to meeting you," she said, breaking the silence.

"What did you tell him?"

She took a moment to answer. "I said you were the only person I trust like him."

This surprised Kyd, but he found women were better at separating the personal from the practical than men. "I hope that's a good thing," Kyd said. His attempt to lighten the mood fell flat. He was back in Moscow sitting next to Irina, but in a surreal dimension, floating. He reminded himself he was suffering jet lag, everything was in stop-motion. He was at the top of a roller coaster without the climb up, teetering, waiting for his gondola to plunge down.

"You look older." She was thinking aloud and surprised when he answered.

"I am older."

"You have family, wife and children?"

"My wife died a few years ago. I have a daughter." He turned to her. "You?"

Her posture stiffened, maybe remembering a lost opportunity. "My brother is more demanding than any husband."

Kyd looked out the side window. He saw a few pedestrians leaning into the blowing snow. "You think your brother can win?"

"Russia needs him to win."

7

"You have deceit in your blood." How was he to interpret this comment? It wasn't easy for Zarefsky to forget, it circled in his brain. He had tough skin, but it was as if Bortnik had found a bruise to poke. At school he had been singled out as different, especially when his mother asked him to honor the Festival of Sacrifice, the Prophet's birthday, or Ramadan. He didn't want to attend, because of the attention it drew, but he obeyed because it pleased his mother. His confrontations at school often ended with tormenters, always more than one, having their noses broken. Of course, it was worse when the teachers made a joke of his Muslim religion and the students laughed. He tried to be a good sport, but laughing was difficult, there was nothing sporting about the torment. The need to fit in led to joining the military. He knew he was valuable and now the president recognized it. While his thoughts circulated, Zarefsky understood he was at a turning point in his career, his life, a make-or-break opportunity. He had been chosen despite all else. If his assignment was successful, he would be rewarded, and religion would be of no consequence. He crouched on a rooftop adjacent to the CPA, with fifty OMOH policemen on the ground floor ready for his command. Major Zarefsky had been told the place and time, and now it was just a matter of waiting. It wasn't for him to question the intelligence, or to understand the politics; his mission was limited to execution. He preferred it this way, there were no gray areas. Zarefsky saw Irina's sedan drive around the building, then watched as it slowed and stopped outside the back entrance as he'd been told it would.

8

THE ENGINE IDLED as Irina spoke Russian into her cell phone. "We're outside." She listened, then turned to Kyd. "Nicoli is waiting for you. You can go inside." She didn't move or turn off the engine.

"You're not coming in?" Kyd asked, surprised.

She looked past him. "I have other business. Once you have the video disk you can take it home." She was edgy.

Kyd wasn't sure what he expected, but it appeared she was eager to be rid of him. A warm reunion might have been too much to hope for, but he thought she would have at least introduced him to her brother. "I'll need a ride to the airport."

She was impatient, anxious. "It's all arranged. Don't worry."

"Like clockwork," he said half to himself. Kyd tried to read her, but couldn't, it had been too long, and she was a different person. He had the sense there was a piece missing, like the itch an amputee feels for a missing leg, but he couldn't figure out what it might be. Kyd followed Irina's eyes to a tall thin shaft of light coming from the building's squinting doorway. Kyd weighed his options, surveying the empty street. Could he return to the airport now, opting out of some clandestine operation he knew was fanciful from the beginning? The snow had thinned to a floating ballet in the headlights. He hadn't made a move to get out, waiting for her to say something more, something that would give him confidence he wasn't making a mistake by continuing.

She spoke to him in Russian. "It was good to see you, Neil."

"Good to see you, too." What more could be said? He was at the top of the roller coaster ready to plunge. Maybe this was his punishment for having left her in the first place, this dangling uncertainty. Didn't he know what he was getting into? Hadn't that been part of his reservation all along? Her eyes were fixed ahead, no doubt on her "other business."

Taking a deep breath, Kyd stepped out onto the footpath, into the razor-sharp wind. It was colder than before, or perhaps he'd become too used to the warm car. Irina sped away, as if escaping, her red taillights fading in the drifting snow. The building's door opened wider, revealing a large man blocking the light. "Come in." It was more of a command than an invitation.

9

WHEN KYD ENTERED the central hall he was empty-handed. After being frisked, Nicoli's guard opened the inner door, hanging on to Kyd's bag like a coat checker. The Archive's main floor was filled with parallel rows of long metal tables with chairs, surrounded by aisles of old books. The tepid, musty odor clung to him. Taking in the Archive, it occurred to Kyd that this was the real Russia—heavy, gloomy and always on the verge of some existential tragedy.

"Nicoli?" Kyd called out, the books swallowing his voice. Why wasn't he welcoming someone who'd traveled halfway around the world to help him?

Nicoli had been watching Kyd from above, appraising Irina's contact. He answered in English, "Up here, my friend." His reply had the cautious enthusiasm of a long-lost relative.

Kyd looked up, spotting his host on the second floor, leaning over the railing. Europeans and Russians called the street level "ground floor," not the first floor, as American's did. Then again, Americans also asked for the "check" in a restaurant rather than the "bill" and insisted on calling the main course an "entrée." Above Nicoli's protruding head was a domed ceiling. It was decorated with a peeling mural depicting some kind of square-jawed scientist peering through a microscope.

The scientist was surrounded by eager students. It was as if the Russian Norman Rockwell had done an inspirational painting using weight lifters as models.

Nicoli pointed from above. "The stairs are against the wall, the elevator doesn't work," he said. This didn't surprise Kyd, a working elevator would have made things too easy. "Just to your left, you'll see them. Good exercise," he instructed, cheerfully.

■

Zarefsky watched as his men surrounded the building, all in riot gear carrying assault rifles. "Block off the streets at one hundred meters," he said to his lieutenant.

The lieutenant, clean-shaven, in his thirties, knew Zarefsky well enough from previous operations and had volunteered to participate. They were both Muslims, and while they never spoke of religion, the lieutenant felt they had a special bond, a bond that would allow him to ride Zarefsky's coattails. "Will they be armed?" he asked.

"Be prepared. We want them captured alive if possible." This wasn't part of Bortnik's orders, but Zarefsky couldn't see the point of murdering without reason, it was wasteful. If the conspirators resisted, he had the authority to shoot.

The lieutenant signaled to the troops, gesturing for them to do as they'd been instructed. Two groups of ten men jogged in opposite directions. The squad had been briefed earlier. They were told it was a confined operation, arresting "enemies of the state," but weren't told who those enemies were. Zarefsky had learned to keep information to a minimum, discouraging personal initiative. He walked around the building, stopping at the door where Kyd had entered. A demolitions officer was quietly attaching an explosive device to the lock.

•

The spiral stairs were rusting iron, creating a soft ringing echo in the cold, moldy stillness as Kyd made his way up. Nicoli Petrov waited for him at the top. He had adopted the politician's handshake, gripping Kyd's hand and forearm at the same time.

Petrov continued with English. "Ah, the famous Mr. Kyd. At last," Nicoli said with a warm smile. Was he talking about getting to Russia, or Kyd's arrival on the second floor? Maybe for politicians everything was too slow.

Kyd retrieved his hand. "Kyd will do."

"Then I'll be Nicoli. After all Irina has told me, I feel we are friends." It was easy to believe his sincerity, although Kyd doubted Irina's report on their "friendship" was comprehensive.

Nicoli noticed Kyd looking around at the groaning shelves. "I come here sometimes when I want to be alone. It's a good place to think." Petrov turned and led Kyd down an aisle where slanting shelves were stuffed with shabby yellowed documents in slumping folders and pancaked boxes. At some stage there had been an attempt at keeping order. Files were labelled in Cyrillic or by numbers with decimal points. "You can find anything in here," Nicoli pointed out.

"Or not." The whole place looked on the verge of collapse.

Nicoli laughed affably. "Yes, quite right, or not."

The musty odor was stifling, as if Kyd had been locked in the closet with a furry sea creature. Nicoli fit in like a piece of living furniture, and having been an academic himself, Kyd understood the gothic charm. If this was where the video disk was hidden, Petrov couldn't do much better.

Nicoli switched to Russian. "You were Irina's linguistics professor I believe?"

"That's right," Kyd responded in Russian.

"And then you became her friend?"

Kyd wasn't sure where any of this was going, but he didn't want to get into a buddy chat. Everything was meant to be worked out beforehand. Kyd figured he could still get to Sheremetyevo Airport by midnight.

"Nicoli, it's nice meeting you, and I wish you well in the election, but I was told you have something for me. Is it here?"

"You also worked for the Central Intelligence Agency?"

"And now I'm a farmer." Why was he stalling?

Petrov's smile widened. "They both involve digging, no?"

Kyd had imagined a handshake, the disk, then the airport. Even the handshake was optional. Kyd's training had taught him preparation was painstaking, execution was fast. The longer an operation took, the more chance something would go wrong. Kyd decided to be blunt. "This needs to be quick, Nicoli. Either you give me the disk or don't. I need to get home."

It was as if Petrov hadn't heard him. He continued walking until he was back at the table where the folded newspaper still lay, next to the atrium. "I want you to know I am not a traitor, I love my country. I want Russia to be a free democratic state …"

The explosion wasn't loud, but a soft body blow, quickly followed by sharp gunfire. Kyd saw the guard that had let him in fall backward as OMOH police marched over him. Their assault rifles pointed in all directions, ready to fire.

Zarefsky, steely confident, stood in the eye of the storm ramrod straight. "Block the exits!" His voice carried the authority of someone never questioned.

Petrov's head swiveled toward Kyd, no sign of the "welcoming relative." "You …"

Kyd guessed the rest of the sentence was something like "… betrayed me!" but Nicoli was stopped by a muffled pop. A small hole appeared in his forehead. He rocked backward, confused, then staggered forward, his body tumbling over the railing in a sloppy somersault, before crashing onto a metal table two floors below. Once his body settled, his eyes stared past Kyd, looking toward the domed ceiling as if seeing it for the first time.

Peripheral movement drew Kyd's attention across the atrium, where he saw an older bald man dressed in the same uniform as the OMOH riot police. He was on his knees, searching for something. The bald man raised his head to see Kyd looking back. He was unconcerned, almost smiling. The commotion around Petrov was growing, and the assassin broke eye contact, collapsing his rifle, and quickly headed toward the stairs.

Zarefsky, standing next to Petrov, traced his fall up to Kyd, still at the railing. The major freed the pistol on his belt.

Without much imagination, Kyd understood he was being set up for Petrov's murder. Why had he been left alive? How had the police known about the meeting and what role had Irina played? Kyd's chances of getting out of Russia had shrunk to a flyspeck-sized target on the horizon. Kyd also knew if he surrendered and survived there was every chance he'd spend the rest of his life in a Russian prison, which wouldn't be surviving at all. It wasn't easy to be logical, hot adrenaline surged through his brain. Kyd ran down the aisle, desperately hoping to find some magical escape hatch—anything. He heard Zarefsky's boot steps climbing the stairs. He was coming up much more quickly than Kyd had.

Painted shut, Kyd bashed the frame of a grimy window with the heel of his hand until it broke free and opened. Sticking his head out into the gusting snow, he saw there was no fire escape or even a ledge. Without wings, he'd end up like Petrov, a bloody rag doll.

Zarefsky's boot steps were becoming louder. He shouted orders. "Begin searching the ground and first floors!" He was not impetuous; he prided himself on being thorough and assured, a man one move from checkmating his opponent. Reaching Kyd's floor, pistol in hand, Zarefsky began walking around the outer rows of shelves, carefully listening for movement.

"Time for surrender. There is no escape." Zarefsky's words were muffled but in English.

Speaking English further confirmed what Kyd had already come to believe, he was a pawn in a covert political game. He needed time to think it through, but there was no time. Kyd looked around the cavernous library, silently praying for help. Not being religious didn't stop him.

"If you resist, I cannot guarantee your safety." Zarefsky's voice was official, matter of fact. "Are you armed?" The major searched one aisle after another, methodically, pointing his revolver ahead like a searchlight. A dim glimmer caught his eye. As he moved closer, he recognized it as a shell casing, discharged onto the third shelf. From where he stood, he had a clear view of where Petrov was shot. He stored the casing in his tunic pocket and continued. One thing at a time.

The lieutenant shouted from below. "Major, the minister is on the phone." Zarefsky knew Bortnik wanted a report, but decided it was better to wait until he could boast the American spy and video disk had been captured.

"I'll call him in a few minutes," Zarefsky replied, walking down the aisle.

There was a dull thud, and the major saw the elevator doors shudder.

Kyd had managed to pull the doors apart, just enough to squeeze through. He remembered stories about frantic parents lifting a car off their child, maybe that's where he got the strength—hopeless desperation. He now stood on a narrow ledge not much wider than the width of his shoe, teetering above the shaft's dark abyss. Kyd worked to calm himself, trying to control his breathing. Once his eyes adjusted, he looked down to see the elevator car far below, in what had to be the basement. There was no telling how long it had been derelict.

Zarefsky's fingers were working through the doors' rubber bumpers, a few inches from Kyd's face. "He's in the elevator shaft. Open it up!" Zarefsky shouted behind him.

Slowly turning his head to the left, Kyd saw the outline of a ladder anchored to the wall. It was too far away to reach with an outstretched arm, but fixed above and between Kyd and the ladder, was a short length of pipe used for electrical wiring. If he could grab the pipe with his right hand, he might be able to swing to the first rung of the ladder. With a heart-thumping clumsy effort, he managed to edge his feet to the right, fingers spidering up the wall.

Zarefsky continued to pull at the doors. "Where can you go? You are in a negative position."

"Negative position?" Kyd mumbled. "Master of the obvious." His fingers gripped the pipe, shifting his weight, ready for the swing to the ladder, when the pipe broke away in his hand. He swayed at the edge, hovering above the shaft, struggling to regain his balance. Kyd pressed back against the doors, and slowly regained his footing, still clenching the pipe as if it were a magic wand.

Zarefsky had separated the doors enough to wedge a foot between them. "It's a long way down," he said, his voice close. Kyd could feel the major's breath on his neck. "Let us help you."

Kyd raised the pipe to shoulder height as the doors opened wider. Positioning the pipe at the opening, he punched it through with all his might, hitting Zarefsky in the face.

"Fuck!" Zarefsky screamed in Russian, his hands disappearing, the doors snapping shut. Two shots rang out. One made it through the rubber jam, whistling past Kyd's ear; the other ricocheted off the door.

There was no time left for considering alternatives—there were none. He dropped the pipe, needing both hands, and heard it clatter and bounce on the elevator car far below. Kyd inched as far right as he could, toward the ladder, knowing he had only one do-or-die chance—if it were a chance at all. No matter how bad things were, he couldn't imagine dying in Russia. How would it even be reported—"American assassin falls to death in failed escape"? There was nothing to hold, and he closed his eyes tight, before refocusing on the ladder, at least a yard from his outstretched hand. He worked to turn both knees in the direction he hoped to jump, and squatted as low as he could without losing his balance. Kyd worked to square his shoulders. He'd never been an athlete, never had that physical ability, but he hoped the power of his desperation would help him fly.

The elevator doors on the first floor were pried open, spilling light into the shaft, making his planned leap look even more suicidal. Kyd had broken into a cold sweat; he dried his hand on his trousers.

A gunshot rang out, fired from below, the bullet shattering masonry next to his head. Kyd moved his right foot halfway off the ledge for an extra push, took a deep breath and dived, arm outstretched, fingers searching, scrapping at empty air, slow, then finding the ladder's bottom rung. He swung for a moment, his fingers slipping until his right hand joined the left. There was no time to exhale, Kyd's weight breaking the ladder loose at the top, bouncing and twisting around the steel cables, wedging between the opposing walls, creating a flimsy diagonal bridge. Kyd dangled from the middle like a zoo monkey.

Zarefsky, cheek bleeding freely, leaned further into the shaft from the first floor and saw Kyd's dark shape swinging from the ladder. He took aim, firing at the hanging target. His shots whizzed around Kyd, and Kyd gave up his grip on the ladder, reaching for the splintered metal cable. He slid down a floor, until the skin on his hands was sawn off, then let go—free-falling, catching a glimpse of Zarefsky's angry, bloody face as he broke through the roof of the elevator car, landing flat on his back. A burst of machine-gun fire followed him, and Kyd dragged his broken body out through the open doors.

Pulling himself upright, the sharp pain in his chest let Kyd guess he'd most likely cracked or broken ribs. The cavernous basement was lit by a single, red emergency lamp attached high on the wall. He could just make out an idle furnace, electrical generator and exposed plumbing running the length of the ceiling. Kyd's adrenaline spike created a confused momentum. He forced himself to slow down and think.

The police were coming, their excited shouts getting louder.

Kyd's eyes scanned the dark room, landing on a heating duct that vented exhaust into the street. He looked around until he found a rusted piece of angle iron lying in the corner, then pushed a box beneath the duct.

Boots were clubbing their way down the stairs.

Balancing on the box, Kyd located a join in the duct he could pry apart with the iron bar. When the join broke and separated, he crawled inside, pulling himself sideways and upward.

The OMOH police had arrived in the basement, their shouts reaching him as if he were trapped in a megaphone. Kyd had made it to street level but was blocked by a thick metal grate. After a feeble try at opening it with damaged hands, Kyd curled around so he could kick it, his ribs grinding. After three jarring attempts the grate gave way. Peering down the street, Kyd could see the riot police gathered at the entrance to the building awaiting orders, while below in the basement, they had discovered the open duct.

"Up here!" The words were followed by gunshots.

Kyd slipped out, crawled, then ran into the darkness.

10

NICOLI PETROV, FORMER presidential candidate, was seated at a table, head lolling to the side, where not long before he had lain like a beached flounder. His newspaper had been retrieved and spread in front of him, opened to the sports pages. The scene suggested Nicoli had been checking the hockey results when he was surprised by a bullet. A policeman, standing behind his chair, was helping Petrov sit upright until rigor mortis could replace him.

Zarefsky, fresh bandage on his cheek, viewed the Petrov drama with distaste, taking instructions on his cell phone. "Not yet, Minister." The sharp voice on the other end could be heard beyond the phone and Zarefsky moved to an isolated corner of the atrium for privacy. A police sentry, waiting with three men near the door, caught Zarefsky's attention and with a wave of his hand, he invited them inside. They carried lighting equipment and a tripod.

"We've sealed the area. He can't escape," Zarefsky said into his phone.

After the unspoken shock of recognition, the photographer directed his two assistants where to put the lighting and tripod for his camera. The photographer motioned the policeman behind Petrov out of the way, and Petrov remained as positioned.

"They've just arrived ..." Zarefsky watched the news crew prepare. "As you say, Minister." The photographer began taking pictures, choreographing different angles.

■

A small entourage had gathered in Irina's living room. They were all friends buoyed by the promise of Nicoli's election. Someone had opened French champagne, the bubbles complementing their high hopes.

Irina had excused herself, she told the others she was exhausted. Up since early morning, planning, preparing, anticipating, they all understood. Nicoli counted on her. Irina lay face up on her bed, mesmerized by the shadows fluttering above her on the ceiling. Seeing Kyd brought up old memories. He wasn't the man she remembered, the erect, light-hearted, confident professor from her past, her lover. Of course, she expected changes with the passing of time, but there was a weight inside him, ballast that held him down, she could see it. Irina still remembered him pacing in front of the class, his enthusiasm contagious and sexy. Neither the difference in their positions or ages had dissuaded her. Irina had booked private consultations for extra help, that was her strategy. He enjoyed speaking Russian with her. Kyd had never visited her homeland, but his accent was as if he were a Muscovite. He had that gift. She invited him to meet some of her Russian friends for dinner, and when her friends left early—they had been instructed to do so—she had him to herself. They spoke about her family, and he told her about his. She took his arm as they walked, and he didn't pull away. The first night they slept together was awkward, the ethical considerations of a student-teacher love affair made him nervous, but with her steadfast persuasion, he soon gave in. They would meet regularly in his sunny apartment. After her father died and she'd returned to Moscow, she asked him to join her. She wanted him to see Russia through her eyes. The first months were bliss, but then he became restless and critical. Their disagreements became more heated, and he became more American. They stopped having sex, or when they did, it felt like another argument. He told her he could never see Russia as home. He'd already bought his ticket back to the US. Irina asked if he loved her and he paused, as if delivering a fatal diagnosis. "It's not easy." After a few months, his emails started to arrive, asking how she was and talking about his life in Washington. He told her he'd taken a job with the CIA, a "pencil pusher" as he described it. She didn't reply. She couldn't forgive him for leaving, or herself for her ridiculous infatuation. Then the emails stopped; he'd met someone. Even after so many years, scratching beneath the surface, there was that connection, that tug from the past that couldn't be forgotten. Despite everything, she did trust him; he'd come back because she asked.

A shrill cry from the living room broke into her thoughts.

When Irina joined the others, they were standing in front of her TV. Irina pushed between her friends to see the news bulletin. She learned her brother had been assassinated—by an American spy. Her legs couldn't hold her, passing out in supportive hands.

11

Kyd had scrambled from doorway to alley, dodging police, crouched and in pain, his chest wheezing as if he were sucking air through a broken harmonica. There was no time to think, the shouts of police pushed him to the edge of a wide-open promenade, separating him from Sokolniki Park. Kyd's memory of the park had come from spending a few Sunday afternoons with Irina and her friends two decades earlier. It was expansive and wooded, with a playground, skating rink, canals, and hiking paths. He didn't expect much had changed. Peering around the sharp corner of a building, Kyd saw a truckload of soldiers joining a group of police half a football field away. He reasoned if he could make it into the park, his pursuers would have to widen their search, their ranks would thin and maybe he could slip through. Slipping through to where remained a mystery but waiting for the noose to tighten around his neck wasn't much of an alternative.

As the groups of police and soldiers attempted to organize their search and figure out who was in charge, Kyd took a pained breath and stepped out from the alley.

As soon as he took a first step, the streetlights seemed to brighten, making him an easy target. He walked at a steady unrushed pace, trying to look like a normal citizen with nothing better to do than stroll through a deserted park in the middle of a subfreezing night. This only worked for about twenty steps.

"Look! There he is!" a soldier shouted. All the others turned in Kyd's direction.

Kyd casually raised a hand and waved to let the soldiers know he was harmless, but they weren't in the mood for a friendly exchange, no doubt smelling a promotion.

"Stop! Stop where you are!" they ordered.

Kyd broke into a run and a burst of machine-gun fire blasted the pavement behind him. His pursuers were faster, but he was closer to the first stand of trees. Reaching the woods, Kyd paused to suck in air. It felt like he was breathing broken glass. The excited shouts were getting closer, light beams bouncing all around him. Kyd was blocked by a frozen pond, something he hadn't remembered. Running either way was a lost cause, there were too many of them and he didn't have the stamina. He moved to the water's edge and tested the thickness of the ice to see if it would hold his weight. The soldiers had become clear silhouettes. Kyd stomped on the edge of the pond and the ice broke away. The lights brushed his face as he lowered himself down to his hands and knees. Kyd held what breath he had and slid beneath the ice, feet first. The water stung but averaged out the pain in his chest and hands. He found a pocket of air created by a dead branch, just large enough for his nose and mouth. The police arrived as opaque images. The officer ordered his men to split up and they took off like bloodhounds, in opposite directions, barking at each other. The commanding officer stood above Kyd, his light glancing off trees and ice, then lingering on Kyd's face. Kyd closed his eyes, preparing for the inevitable shot, when the officer's radio crackled to life. "He's entered Sokolniki Park, we're in pursuit."

Kyd's breath was becoming more labored; his lungs wanted to expand, trapped within the broken bars of his rib cage. It wasn't hard for him to imagine being pulled from the pond as an ice sculpture.

He heard the radio response. "Shoot to kill."

The officer strode away, light vanishing.

When Kyd pulled himself out of the pond, his wet clothes stiffened to frost. He had to keep moving. Kyd forced himself to stand, walking then scuffling deeper into the park. The police flashlights became an obstacle course of lighthouse warnings.

Kyd jogged through the fairground, around the Ferris wheel and past the small dark kiosks that sold food during the summer. At the edge of Sokolniki, his feet and hands numb blocks of ice, Kyd watched a police car idle next to a bakery van. The baker shook his head, and the car cruised on. When the baker took a tray of bread from the back of the van and entered a café, Kyd scrambled across the street, opening the van's back doors, climbing inside. Getting out of the freezing cold and near the warm bread allowed Kyd to take a sharp pained breath, but he couldn't stop shaking. The metal trays rattled like tinny snare drums. He yelled at himself, "Stop! Stop, goddamn it!" His body didn't obey. Crawling as close to the front as possible, hidden by the shelves, Kyd willed himself to become invisible. The driver returned, replaced the empty trays, and closed the doors.

The baker hadn't driven more than five minutes when he stopped for another delivery. Kyd waited at the doors, and when they opened, he jumped out and ran the best he could, his arms and legs moving like frozen dough.

As the sky lightened, Kyd found a clothing store. Shivering uncontrollably, he walked to the display window, where he could see a wide variety of winter clothes. He used his elbow to break the glass at the entrance and opened the door, immediately setting off a screeching alarm. He figured he had at least five minutes to get what he needed. Inside, Kyd quickly rummaged through the clothes carrousels and shelves, grabbing a coat, flannel shirt, pants, socks and boots. He only had time to guess the sizes. He snatched a scarf, knit hat and gloves. Sirens were approaching.

Kyd ducked behind the store, hiding himself in the loading dock's dark recess, and began undressing. He treated it as an Olympic event. His skin had turned blue, not a pretty blue, more like bruised meat. His chest ached, and the effort of raising his arms caused him to scream into his elbow. The sirens were close, and Kyd was certain the quick response was because they knew he was the thief. They would soon be joined by others, creating an inescapable net. After he'd managed to put on his dry socks, shirt, coat and pants, he tried on his boots. They were a surprising fit. The beanie and scarf almost completed his new wardrobe. He waited to put on one of his gloves until he'd searched his wet, discarded clothes. Kyd grabbed his money and cell phone, everything else had been left in his bag. The phone, waterlogged, was useless, but he needed the SIM card. There was still something stiff wedged in his soggy shirt pocket. He slipped his fingers in and pulled out Boris' business card.

12

AN AIRPORT SECURITY agent sat in front of his computer, scrolling through columns of US passport photos, recent arrivals. The major's muscular presence loomed over his narrow shoulders like an anvil ready to fall. "There," Zarefsky said, identifying the face he'd seen through the elevator doors. Zarefsky lifted his hand to feel the wound on his cheek.

The agent selected and enlarged the image of "Douglas Reynolds." The major bent further forward and studied the information, pointing at a green dot in the upper left corner of the screen. "What's this?" His deep voice resonating in the agent's ear.

OMOH alone was intimidating, but the major's close presence caused the agent's voice to tremble. "He was flagged."

Zarefsky straightened and moved sideways to face the agent. "Flagged, why?"

The agent chose not to meet the major's eyes. "We were ordered to report his arrival."

"Ordered by whom?"

The agent squirmed. "I don't know, higher-up. It wasn't my decision." He hoped the major would take a step back.

Zarefsky stared at the man for a moment, as if a human lie detector, then moved past him. Of course the agent hadn't been told who or why; information was valuable, not to be given away. There was a large observation window allowing a second-floor view of the airport's entry hall, where new flight arrivals met customs officials. Zarefsky could normally pick the nationality of each arrival merely by the way they were dressed or the way they comported themselves, but he gazed through the window observing nothing. His surroundings faded into blank wallpaper as he gathered his thoughts. If "higher-ups" knowingly allowed the American into the country, wouldn't that mean they had encouraged the encounter? The meeting between Petrov and Reynolds had not been uncovered by the government, it had been orchestrated. Zarefsky had now become infected by information he shouldn't have, making him a reluctant co-conspirator. He shook his head, hoping to clear it, or better, redirect his thinking. His primary goal was to capture or kill the American and letting his thoughts stray beyond that was dangerous. Knowledge came with responsibility.

When he turned around, he saw all eyes were on him, waiting for instruction. His lieutenant stood near the door. Zarefsky directed him, "Print the photo and see that it is distributed to every police station in Moscow. If anyone suspects they've seen this man, have them contact you directly. Understood?"

The lieutenant responded with a salute in his voice. "Understood."

With this assurance, Zarefsky walked out, aiming to outdistance his suspicions.

13

TWENTY YEARS EARLIER, Kyd had visited the US Embassy to help solve a visa renewal issue. He had needed a sponsor for his Russian Letter of Invitation. Irina was his sponsor. A day wasted standing in lines, repeatedly answering the same questions and filling in forms no one would ever read. He counted on the embassy being in the same location, but who knew how things might have changed? If he managed to get inside, he'd be protected, sacred ground. He would wait there until the geniuses who put him in his present position found a way of getting him home. He'd gone above and beyond what could be expected, above and beyond what could even be explained, certainly meeting the requirement of "genuine effort." They'd thrown him into a shark tank and somehow, through CIA training, blind luck, and Boy Scout perseverance, he'd survived. People had the wrong idea about spies, they weren't James Bond or able to turn a coffee mug into a satellite dish like in the movies. They were trained in detection and self-preservation. Nicoli's disk wasn't more important than his life and they had to accept that. Kyd had walked miles, unable to risk public transport, forced to change routes several times to avoid the roving soldiers and police cars. If he paused to think about it, his situation couldn't be more unreal. No more than three days earlier he had been banging on Margaret's tractor. Now he was an American assassin running from Russian police, suffering the effects of jet lag, exhaustion, and a wrecked body. When had he last slept or eaten? He couldn't remember. At the very least, the embassy owed him a decent meal and warm bed.

Poking his head out of an alleyway, he saw the US flag fluttering above the embassy, still in the same place, but his relief was short-lived. Below the flag, surrounding the embassy's perimeter, were platoons of circling police. Of course, they were on heightened alert, checking the IDs of anyone within a block of the entrance. It would be impossible for Kyd to get close, much less enter. Why had he expected anything else? He was the suspect in a political assassination. Kyd leaned back against the building's brick facade, exhausted by futility. What would he do now? What was his plan? His brain wasn't working properly. Wishing circumstances were different or easier was wasted energy. He teased himself with the possibility of surrender, walking out into the open, gifting some soldier a prize. Or, would he endure, putting one foot in front of the other until he ran out of hope? He had never thought of himself as an endurance guy, more the guy who got along, the guy who was prepared and ready to work. His tired brain searched for inspiration. There was Reinhold Messner who climbed to the summit of Everest without oxygen, and there was Olly Hicks, who rowed a boat, solo, from America to England. How had they coped? What kept them going? Would they give up in this situation? And, there was Molly Kyd, an eleven-year-old girl who endured more senseless pain than he could even imagine. Molly Kyd—his daughter that had faith in him. Wasn't that enough incentive to continue? His chest objected every time he breathed harder than a parakeet, but he had to find his way home. Whining wouldn't get him anywhere, he needed to take control.

Without any medical training, Kyd was aware he needed to strap his ribs to still the movement. He remembered this from a TV soap he had watched with Patty. She loved doctor shows where impossible diseases found miracle cures. Kyd searched the streets until he found the green cross that advertised a Russian pharmacy. Before going in, he pulled his stocking cap down to just above his eyes and wrapped his scarf to cover the lower part of his face. Once inside, he skirted the checkout counter to grab rolls of elastic bandage, gauze, tape, scissors, and antiseptic ointment for his hands. His ribs had taken his mind off his mangled hands, stiff with dried blood.

He clocked a plump, gray-haired babushka finishing a call on her cell phone, dropping it into her large shoulder bag. She shuffled to the counter and Kyd stood behind her. Both the store clerk and the customer were distracted by a TV mounted on a shelf above the counter. President Garin stood at a podium, looking somber.

"What's happened?" the babushka asked.

"Petrov's been murdered," the storekeeper replied.

The woman gasped and looked at Kyd to see if he shared her astonishment.

"Terrible," Kyd mumbled.

She turned her attention back to the screen, listening to what the president had to say. Garin seemed on the edge of tears. "Last night Russia lost a great patriot, Nicoli Petrov."

Kyd dipped his hand into the shopper's shoulder bag and retrieved her cell phone, slipping it into his coat pocket.

Garin continued, "While we were political opponents, I admired him greatly and this government will not rest until his assassin is brought to justice." Garin, unable to control his emotions, left the podium, his image replaced by a studio news reporter.

"Police say they are looking for this man, an American calling himself Douglas Reynolds."

Kyd was shocked to see his passport photo on TV. He had hoped identification would take longer. The shopkeeper and customer slowly turned to Kyd, who left a pile of notes on the counter, quickly walking out with his medical supplies.

14

WEXLER WASN'T SURPRISED to be called into Sorrow's office, he expected it. He sat in a straight-backed chair, legs crossed at the knees, patient. Clyde Sorrow was behind his desk. Wexler wore one of his customary tailored suits, not to intimidate, although he was okay with it, but to project confidence. He had found a brilliant Italian tailor in Trenton, New Jersey, who knew his taste in style and fabric. Fine clothes weren't cheap, but he thought of them as music for the body. His boss, on the other hand, dressed in what Wexler could only assume he'd bought off the rack at Best For Less. Sorrow, a few years younger than Wexler's fifty-two, was slumped in his desk chair. The president's photographic portrait on the wall behind him, peered over Sorrow's shoulder like a bride's father. Wexler brushed an invisible speck off the thigh of his trousers as Sorrow took a moment to polish his glasses with a small square microfiber cloth. They had spent weeks gaming the operation with various departments, both covert and overt, analyzing and discussing the message that had arrived despite the two dead couriers. Should they proceed? Shouldn't they proceed? What were the reasonable gains against the risks? At one point it seemed the whole idea would be scrapped and now it was active. The CIA was all about plans and plans within plans. It was very easy to lose sight of the forest in the trees.

Sorrow leaned back in his squeaky chair, replacing his lopsided glasses. "So, Paul, what have we?" There was no point in answering, Sorrow wanted to be heard. He drummed his pen on the desktop, building to a crescendo. "It seems we have a renegade, quasi-spy farmer who outwits the Russian police with or without the chemical weapons evidence we want." He paused, the glare from the overhead light on Sorrow's lenses prevented Wexler from seeing his eyes. "Does he have the evidence, Paul?" There was a rumor, undocumented, that before Sorrow came to the CIA, he managed his family's international "small meats" business.

"He's on the run, we haven't heard." Wexler thought this was obvious, but added, "Dancing lessons from God." He knew Sorrow was fond of platitudes, vanilla being his flavor of choice.

Sorrow tilted his head back and smiled. "'Dancing lessons from God.' Not original, I assume?"

"It could be, I can't remember." Of course he could remember, he was paraphrasing Kurt Vonnegut.

"I like that. It gives weight to the unexpected." His gaze returned to Wexler. "There's concern, Paul." His index finger pointed up, under the president's jaw. "We need the evidence." Sorrow leaned forward, close enough for Wexler to smell his stale breath. "We know you won't let us down."

Wexler didn't need a lesson on the laws of gravity, shit always rolled downhill. He stood, buttoning his coat. "Leave it with me."

15

KYD DID AS much as he could to hide his face. Using back alleys, he kept his head down and wore the scarf and stocking cap. Now that he had the supplies, it was a matter of finding a safe place to repair his body. Kyd found a single closet toilet near a food stall. Locked inside, he struggled to remove his coat and shirt within the close space. Looking in the small mirror above the basin, he saw the right side of his rib cage was a vivid purple. Kyd unspooled the elastic bandage and wrapped it around his chest three times, as tightly as possible, given his limited flexibility. Even the effort of lifting his arms halfway was excruciating. With some difficulty, he managed to get his shirt back on. Kyd tugged off his gloves and the dried blood came off with them. His palms began to bleed again. He used the gauze to dab his bloody hands with ointment, then used the scissors to cut off the gloves' fingers. This would protect his wounds and allow him to pick up a *kopek*.

There was pounding on the door and a husky voice shouted, "What the fuck are you doing in there? Get out!" The angry banging continued, but looking in the mirror, Kyd had an idea. He took the bloody gauze he'd used on his hands and folded it into a large square, taping it over the center of his face. The bandage made it look like he'd broken his nose but also worked as a mask.

"Get out of there or I'm going to push this thing over!" The banger was trying to force the door open, rocking the toilet.

Kyd put on his coat and beanie, pulling it down over his forehead, before unlocking the door. He was greeted by a burly police sergeant, who grabbed Kyd by the shirt and yanked him out, practically throwing him into the arms of his jeering comrade. The sergeant slammed the door after himself and Kyd, helped by a kick, stumbled away.

There was a chest-high hedge next to a playground, shielding him from the street. Kyd pulled his waterlogged cell phone out of his pocket, dislodged the SIM card, and installed it in the stolen phone. He called an implanted number, then was asked for a code he'd memorized. A short, shrill signal sounded before he could speak. "I need you to get me out of here." Kyd was confident they'd call him back with a prepared plan—"Go to this address, it's a safe house, we'll get you out." Something like that. They had to have a plan if things went bad; after all, they were the CIA, the most devious and sophisticated spy organization on Earth. As he waited, and looked over the hedge, he could see a small huddle of mothers staring at him. They held their kids close. Kyd, the parent, got it. He was a disheveled single man who looked like he'd escaped a washing machine filled with razor blades.

A cheerful show tune sounded on his new phone, a gift from the previous owner. It was Wexler. "Are you safe?" he asked.

"I'm a TV star. You need to get me out of here." Kyd tried not to shout.

"Do you have the video disk?"

The mothers were soliciting a father's opinion, who'd arrived with his daughter. The mothers pointed at Kyd, and the father, overweight but tall, looked over at the shady voyeur hiding on the other side of the hedge. The newcomer was ready to be a hero.

Kyd stayed on the phone with Wexler, while keeping an eye on the hero. He was on his way over. "The embassy's surrounded, I'm a sitting duck."

Wexler was unreasonably calm, as Kyd imagined an airplane pilot might be before a crash—"Make sure to fasten your seat belt." He told Kyd, "We're going to get you out, but we need the video disk. Do you have it?"

It didn't seem Wexler could read the panic in Kyd's voice. "Fuck the disk, Paul. Petrov's dead, the disk doesn't matter anymore." There was no immediate reply and Kyd thought the connection might have been broken. "Wexler?"

Wexler's voice remained steady. "We need the disk."

The father was close, Kyd could see his furrowed brow and hands curling into fists. The mothers hugged their children tighter. Kyd put his phone away, dodging traffic to cross a busy street. The hero father stopped on the other side, deciding if he should follow.

Wexler, in his office with Barnes, shouted into his cell. "Kyd, you there?" His impatience grew. "Kyd?" The line was dead, and he let his hand drop. "Damn it!" He didn't want to admit it but depending on Kyd in any circumstance grated on his ego. At the heart of it was Patty's rejection. How could she have chosen him?

Barnes looked at Wexler from her position near the door. "Does he have it?"

"How the hell would I know?" Wexler worked at getting his anger under control. As with his clothes, he believed reserve projected strength. "He didn't say. He wants us to pull him out."

"What do you want to do?" she asked.

"We'll wait for him to make contact again." He looked at Barnes and forced a smile. "It's a miracle he's still in play."

Barnes had another question that had been on her mind. "How did they know about the meeting?"

Wexler gave her the simple answer. "Someone snitched."

Kyd saw the father reporting back to the mothers and receiving congratulations. He soaked it up in manly fashion, glancing back toward Kyd, who was making his way down the street. Kyd couldn't wander aimlessly. It was too dangerous. It would be foolhardy to assume the mothers hadn't reported him to the police. He paused in a doorway, reached into his pocket, and found Boris' card.

Kyd spoke in Russian with an almost giddy voice. "I was given your number by a friend, and he said you're a great guide. I will pay top rates." He listened to Boris for a moment. "Now ..."

16

ZAREFSKY AND HIS lieutenant shared an elevator taking them down to the mortuary. Zarefsky stood a step ahead of the other officer, facing his own blurred reflection in the stainless-steel doors. His descent to the morgue seemed appropriate. He was now on a loser's mission, opportunity turned into misfortune. Even when he captured Reynolds, and he had no doubt he would, Zarefsky would only be remembered for having let him get away. To the government, he was fixing his mistake. Every time he touched the small bandage beneath his right eye he was reminded of his failure. He had been a rising star and now he wasn't. He had been a faithful husband, now he wasn't. Sofia would not come back to him, he was resigned to that. Earlier in the day, she had delivered the final papers for their divorce. She looked happy, having found her "joy." Zarefsky couldn't guess if this new spark was fanned by someone else, or just being free of him. "How long has it been bad?" he asked her. "Years?" But she turned away, relieved to have the end in sight. He'd lost his center. What or who could he count on? Work was all he had left.

"We have troops around the US Embassy," the lieutenant said, breaking the silence. This was expected, but he was never comfortable with Zarefsky's dark moods. They seemed like a slow, cold burning fuse, foreshadowing an imminent explosion. The fuse had burned since Reynolds's escape.

Zarefsky spoke to his reflection. "Airports and train stations?"

"Police are there with Reynolds's photograph," the lieutenant replied.

The doors slid open and Zarefsky stopped them from closing with his foot, blocking the lieutenant's exit. "What about Reynolds's weapon, the weapon he used for the assassination? Have you found it in the building?"

"He must have taken it with him, maybe down the shaft."

"If he had a weapon, why didn't he use it? Search again," Zarefsky ordered.

The doors closed, the lieutenant left inside.

Irina stood beside Nicoli, his body face-up on a mortuary gurney. A shroud covered all but his head. To her, his lifeless body resembled a discarded costume, she felt no attachment to the empty shell—whoever her brother was, he had left. Make-up did little to hide the bullet hole in his forehead.

Movement stirred the room and she turned to see two policemen near the door stand to attention as Zarefsky entered. He took off his hat, holding it against his heart as a sign of respect. She noticed the stars resting on his broad shoulders.

"Ms. Petrov, I am sorry for your loss," he offered.

Irina quickly assessed Zarefsky, judging a book by its cover— "meat and potatoes," another self-important brute. "It's Russia's loss," she corrected.

"I'm Major Zarefsky, with OMOH. I will be leading the investigation into your brother's death."

"Assassination," she corrected again.

"I have a couple questions, if you wouldn't mind?" He took in her austere appearance, understandably different from the effervescent personality he'd seen from Bortnik's balcony. He had seen her as supplementary, but now recognized strength in her defiance. Tragedy had added to her beauty.

"Can I stop you?" she asked.

His heavy tanklike presence made it clear she couldn't. "Do you know why your brother was at the CPA?"

"He sometimes went there to be alone, to think." She emphasized the word *think* as if it might be a foreign concept to him.

"Yes, very quiet, private. He never mentioned meeting someone?" He pulled at a loose thread he noticed on his sleeve, snapping it off.

"As I said, he went there to be alone." Her impatience was becoming obvious.

Zarefsky remained calm, polite. "Ah, but didn't you deliver someone there, an American?"

Now that she looked into his eyes, she realized she had underestimated this man. He had a wolf's cunning. She took a step back. "Are you accusing me of something?"

"Major ..." An older man, bald, who Zarefsky hadn't noticed before, approached from a corner of the room. Zarefsky held up his hand like a traffic warden, stopping him from getting closer.

"Major, Ms. Petrov is grieving. Surely, she can be interrogated later."

Zarefsky assessed this new presence, unused to having his behavior questioned. "Who are you?"

"I was sent by Minister Bortnik to protect Ms. Petrov," the bald man answered.

"Whom are you protecting her from?" Zarefsky wouldn't have been surprised to hear his own name.

"Perhaps the minister can answer your question."

The major pulled his attention back to Irina, advancing on the space she'd given up. He spoke in a low voice only she could hear, confidentially. "Tell me where he is."

Irina took a second step back. "I have no idea what you're talking about." She looked over his shoulder, as if planning an escape.

"Yes, rest. We'll talk again," Zarefsky said. Then he turned to the bald man, taking in his bloodless face, assuming the mortuary was where he felt most at home.

17

BORIS WAS WELL acquainted with what tourists wanted—visits to the Kremlin, Red Square and St. Basil's Cathedral were routine. If they were willing to pay for the evening, there were restaurants and clubs. He had friends and friends of friends who would make their night special. Often, these foreign tourists, with a little encouragement, invited Boris to join them as a guest interpreter. Russian tourists weren't nearly so generous, coming to the big city from small towns and farms. Most had only read about Moscow in books. Boris had made up his mind, he was through working for politicians, being a taxi for killers was not something he wanted on his resume. When he paused to think about it, from the beginning he could see Reynolds was a killer. His eyes were steely cold. Was he really talking to his daughter, or was it some kind of spy code? Never again, no matter how much they paid. He wanted to see his kids grow up. Boris had cruised around the block twice, in heavy traffic, exhausting his cigarettes, cursing, looking for the promised fare. Each time he'd circled around, his quoted price doubled. The tourist wasn't where he said he'd be, and Boris suspected his time could be better spent on lunch. Unfortunately, he wasn't in a position to turn down work, his wife wanted another baby. It wasn't an argument he could win if he ever wanted sex again. He would go around one last time. Boris was forced to stop behind a delivery truck, and before he had a chance to honk his horn twice, his back door opened. He turned to see his passenger, and even with the large bandage covering his nose, Boris recognized him immediately. The first thought he had was *What a coincidence!* While he tried to make sense of the odd occurrence, Kyd put the point of his sharp scissors to Boris' throat.

"Drive," Kyd ordered in Russian.

"You speak Russian?"

"Drive, Boris."

Boris nosed his car past the delivery truck and entered the traffic.

Kyd spoke into his ear. "Turn at the next street and find a quiet place to park."

Boris turned the corner, into a smaller street. He switched to English. "Please, we are friends, I have family. I know nothing."

"Pull over and turn off the engine," Kyd commanded.

Boris found a place to park. "I don't believe what they say, I am good judge of humans." The fear in his voice betrayed his sincerity.

"Lock your door." Kyd didn't want Boris to take a chance. He dutifully pushed down the button. Kyd saw a shiny new car pull out of an industrial garage ahead, but otherwise, the street was quiet. "I want to speak to Irina Petrov." If she gave him the video disk, he could use it as leverage to get out. Wasn't that the plan from the beginning?

"I drive, nothing else," Boris told him.

Kyd made sure Boris was aware of the scissors, denting his neck with the point. "Boris, I'm a desperate man, a man who has nothing to lose. Do you understand what that means?"

Boris was sweating. "You don't mind hurting me."

"Yes, that's what I'm saying. Who hired you to pick me up at the airport? I'll know if you're lying."

The point of the scissors pressed harder, and Boris spoke quickly. "My friend, Peter. He works for Petrov. It is only my good English they hire me. This is the truth, no lying." Boris crossed himself to add credibility.

"Call Peter and tell him Mr. Reynolds wants to speak with Irina Petrov."

"Yes, sure. It is more easy for me to speak without point." Boris' eyes were large in the mirror.

When Kyd withdrew the scissors, a dot of blood appeared on Boris' neck. In Russian, Kyd told him, "Say only what I've told you, nothing more. Think of your family."

Boris retrieved his cell and punched in a number. "Peter, it's me ... Listen, Peter! Mr. Reynolds wants to speak to Irina Petrov ... Yes, he's with me now ..."

Kyd could hear Peter's excited voice on the other end, but Kyd pushed Boris to keep going.

"Listen!" Boris insisted.

Kyd put his lips close to Boris' ear. "Is Peter a good friend of yours?"

Boris nodded. "Yes, I think so."

"Tell him if he doesn't do as I ask, I'll kill you."

Looking into Kyd's crazed eyes, Boris didn't doubt it. "Peter, he will kill me if you don't do this." Peter's muffled reaction could be heard from the other end.

Kyd took out his cell phone and showed Boris the number. "Tell him to give her this."

"Here's the number for her to call." Boris read the number into the phone.

Kyd took Boris' phone and turned it off. "Now we wait."

Irina sat in front of her television as the Russian president's initial address was rebroadcast in a fuller version. It had evolved into more of a campaign speech than a eulogy. Garin's crocodile tears were the theatrics of an amateur thespian. How long had he practiced it in front of a mirror? Perhaps he was practicing it before Nicoli was murdered.

Her new bodyguard, sent by the minister, stood against the wall, between her and the door, blank-faced. He had introduced himself as Anton Tarkoff. She had never seen him sit, his head gleamed as if it were polished, and if she'd been told he was a mechanical invention, she might have believed it. Irina had no illusions about why he was present, she only waited for what might happen next. Major Zarefsky's questions had unnerved her. If they knew about the meeting, they would probably know about the disk.

A knock at her door broke into her thoughts. Tarkoff went to answer, and she could hear the exchange.

"What do you want?" Tarkoff asked.

"I have a message for Ms. Petrov."

Irina looked behind her and vaguely recognized Peter, a tall skinny man with tousled hair wearing a neat sports coat. He had been one of the fresh-faced volunteers Nicoli preferred. "They're idealistic and ambitious," he told her. "They are the fuel we need to win." The young volunteers spent hours at the election office, photocopying and running errands, laughing and discussing the future with Nicoli as president.

Tarkoff blocked his path inside. "She's resting. You can tell me."

Peter stammered, "Mr. Reyn ... Mr. Reynolds wants her to call him."

"Where is he?" Tarkoff's interest grew.

"With my friend."

"Give me his number."

Peter balked at the bodyguard, looking past him, toward Irina, who had moved near the door. "It's a message for Irina," Peter insisted.

"Let him in," Irina said.

Tarkoff considered, then stepped aside, allowing Peter to enter.

Peter, face to face with Irina, lowered his eyes. "Your brother was a tremendous inspiration to me."

She nodded. "You have a phone number?"

The bald man moved closer. "I'll deal with this."

"He's threatening to kill my friend if you don't call," Peter explained.

Irina pulled the note out of Peter's hand before Tarkoff could grab it. Picking up her phone off the coffee table, she walked into her bedroom and closed the door.

Tarkoff turned to the young man. "What's your friend's name?"

"Boris Khrushchev."

Tarkoff smiled, putting a reassuring hand on Peter's shoulder. "Don't worry, we will help your Mr. Khrushchev."

Peter nodded, unsure, looking toward Irina's closed door.

In her bedroom, Irina spoke softly into her phone. "Say something so I know it's you."

Kyd leaned forward in his seat and thought for a moment, watching Boris' nervous glances. "You have a birthmark on your left hip. Where can we meet?" Kyd listened, then responded, "Only you, no one else."

Kyd ended the call. He looked at the cars driving past on the cross street. There seemed to be more police cars, or maybe he imagined it.

Boris couldn't help himself. "You know Irina well."

"I'm meeting her this evening. I'll need somewhere safe to wait." Kyd found Boris' eyes in the rear-view mirror. "Where do you live?"

18

BORIS' APARTMENT WAS cramped and had the tangy odor of cabbage soup mixed with cigarette smoke. No doubt his family had spent the winter with windows closed to preserve the heating. In the living room, a threadbare couch, no nicer than Margaret's, had bright embroidered pillows and was flanked by two shabby lounge chairs. Toys littered the floor and an empty pizza box lay open on the coffee table. Kyd got the impression the Khrushchevs lived in a rush.

"Do you have a phone charger?" Kyd needed to call Molly. Without a miracle, he couldn't see himself getting back in time for her treatments, a promise broken.

"On the table." Boris pointed to a wooden pedestal stand in the corner, where he'd put his keys.

With feigned sincerity, Boris added, "Yes, of course, my home is your home." There was still the chance Reynolds wouldn't kill him if he was friendly. "You want to listen to music? I have big collection." He picked up a few toys from the floor but didn't know where to put them. He tossed them on the couch. "TV works." He took a cigarette from a new pack he found on a shelf, then opened the window a fraction and lit up. "You will be safe here."

Kyd looked around—pictures on the wall, a few holiday souvenirs, Boris' well-thumbed Russian-English dictionary.

Boris bent down to blow smoke out the window. It didn't make much difference. "Wife doesn't like smoking in house," Boris explained, as if he were playing a trick on her.

Kyd looked at the family photo on the wall, the same one in Boris' car, only larger. "When do they get home?"

"Sometimes five, sometimes before. They are at my mother's. My mother likes kids." He noticed Kyd's drooping eyes. "You want to lie down, rest a little, there is time?"

Kyd could feel the last forty-eight hours catching up with him. He'd been running a marathon, and now that he paused, every muscle in his body seemed to sag. His chest had never stopped aching, but he could tune it out as long as adrenaline had pushed him forward. "Do you have coffee?" Kyd asked.

"I can make."

"Make," Kyd answered. Maybe caffeine could keep him going. If he didn't get a boost soon, he'd collapse.

Kyd followed Boris down the hallway past a kids' room with unmade beds and colorful posters of pop stars.

The kitchen was small, dirty dishes filled the sink. There was a pot of something on the stove, maybe cabbage soup.

"Sorry the mess." Boris shrugged.

"Make the coffee strong," Kyd directed.

Boris found a small aluminum espresso maker in the pile of unwashed dishes. "Will only take a minute. You can sit," he said, giving the assassin permission. Boris paused to look at Kyd. "Excuse me for saying, but you don't look so excellent."

"You're observant," Kyd admitted.

"Yes, only saying." Boris added water to the machine.

Kyd took advantage of the chair beside a chipped, laminated breakfast table, intent on staying awake. He watched Boris, cigarette smoldering in his mouth, nervously spilling coffee grounds. Kyd pulled the gauze from his nose. "Relax, Boris. Just don't do anything stupid." Boris turned to look at him. Kyd added, "I didn't kill anyone." He worked hard to stay upright, propping an elbow on the table.

Boris considered. "I don't believe so. You are good friends with Irina." Boris looked through the refrigerator. "No milk, but I have strong vodka." He proudly pointed to a bottle on a small shelf next to the stove. "A gift from customer." The phone in Boris' pocket vibrated and he looked toward Kyd. His guest was slumped on the table, head resting on his folded arms. Kyd was asleep.

Boris quietly walked down the hall before he answered in a whisper. "He's here ... At my home, sleeping ... I don't think so ... Yes, of course ..." Boris disappeared into the living room, his voice disappearing with him.

•

Kyd moved through a darkened house, slowly looking in one room after another, but they were all the same, single beds and blank walls, prisonlike. He continued to walk forward, the hallway funneling the walls, ceiling, and floor to a dead end. There was nowhere to go; he was trapped.

"Daddy." Her voice was light and clear.

Kyd turned to see a small figure coming toward him, vague, as if looking through a cataract.

"Daddy." Her voice was louder; it was Molly. Her image sharpened. She shouted, "Daddy, wake up!"

Kyd sat bolt upright, startled awake, trying hard to orient himself. A man had entered the kitchen—the bald man he'd seen murder Nicoli Petrov.

Tarkoff smiled at Kyd as though they were old friends. "You are an important person," he said in English.

"Am I?" Kyd didn't know if he had the strength to stand.

"Give me disk." Tarkoff moved closer.

Kyd stood, his legs jelly. "You killed Petrov before he gave it to me."

The bald man flicked open a knife, arms wide, moving forward, blocking Kyd's way out. "Where is it?"

"I don't know. Like I said, he didn't give it to me." Kyd wondered if Boris might come to his rescue, but on second thought, he knew Boris wasn't a rescuing kind of guy.

"If you don't have the disk, you are useless." Not so different to what Wexler had said.

Kyd scrambled to open a kitchen drawer, hoping to find a knife of his own, but Tarkoff kicked it shut, knocking Boris' bottle of vodka off the shelf. Kyd grabbed the rolling bottle and knocked the neck off on the counter. Undeterred by Kyd's jagged weapon, Tarkoff angled forward, enjoying the game, certain of the outcome. Kyd's back was pressed against the stove. He waited for a chance, cocked his wrist and flung vodka into Tarkoff's eyes. The bald man wiped at the burning liquid as Kyd splattered the rest of the bottle over his head and shoulders. While Tarkoff tried to clear his vision, Kyd pulled a match from the box near the stove. The small flame found the alcohol, the fire quickly climbing up Tarkoff's arm, neck, and head. The bald man dropped his knife, frantically slapping at the flames engulfing him. Tarkoff bounced off the walls, stumbling down the hallway, entering the living room as a human torch. By the time Kyd caught up, he was smothering the fire with a curtain. Kyd grabbed the wooden stand where his phone was charging and brought it down hard on Tarkoff's head. The bald man fell to the floor, silent.

Kyd finally saw Boris, sprawled on the floor, his throat cut. Then, looking up, he recognized Boris' stunned wife and children from the photo, standing in the doorway. He could read her thoughts—her husband drove taxis, how could this happen? Kyd didn't have time to console or explain, even if he could. He grabbed his phone and the keys to Boris' car, pushing past them through the doorway.

No sooner had Kyd left, than Tarkoff struggled to his knees, stood, and staggered past the bewildered family.

19

KYD PARKED BORIS' car on a dark quiet street and tried to sleep in the back. The car still reeked of cigarettes, and despite the cold, he had to leave the windows open. Kyd put one of Boris' dangling pine trees near his face. He'd organized to meet Irina at 7:00, two hours away. At first, Kyd worried if he fell asleep, he might never wake up, but that's not the way it was. Each time he closed his eyes, the images of Nicoli, staring up blankly from two floors below, the assassin's burning face and Boris' stunned wife skipped around in his mind's eye like the colorful frames of an experimental movie. He had to clear his head before he met Irina. Everything revolved around the video disk. When she gave it to him the Agency would find a way to get him out. Even though Irina had set up the meeting with Nicoli, it was hard for him to believe she wanted her brother dead. She was different, but not that different. Kyd was dog-paddling in a deep dark ocean looking for shore.

He drove along the winding course of the Moskva River, the icy surface reflecting the lights of the city. On another night he might have taken in its sparkling beauty, but on this night the entire city seemed a seductive trap. As Kyd approached the statue of Peter the Great, he slowed and picked out a female figure standing apart from the huddled romantic couples and tourists taking photos. Her head and most of her face were covered in a scarf, but he could still recognize her, her composure.

Kyd rolled down his window and called out, "Get in."

Once inside, Irina lowered her scarf and he drove away. Kyd checked the rear-view mirror for anyone following, then realized if a spy wasn't waving a red flag, he wouldn't recognize them anyway.

Kyd wasn't much interested in knowing how or why he was set up, that time had passed. He was blunt. "I need the video disk." When Irina didn't respond, he turned and saw she was pointing a pistol at his chest. "What are you doing?"

"Why?" she asked, her voice cracking like glass. It wasn't hard to fill in the blanks. "Was it the CIA?"

Kyd was baffled. "My mind might be a little hazy, but aren't you the one who brought me here? Why would I kill him? My job was to get the disk and leave." He didn't know why he even had to remind her. She was fidgeting with the gun and Kyd could see her finger on the trigger. "Point that somewhere else." Her aim didn't waver. He pointed out what she had to know. "The police knew everything, they knew when and where we were meeting. The assassin was already there, so I would say it has more to do with you than with me."

"I loved my brother!" Irina screamed.

He could see she was squeezing the trigger, raising the pistol high enough for Kyd to get a clear view down the barrel. He swiped at it, losing control of the car, and swerving in front of oncoming traffic. A deafening shot shattered the windshield as the car jumped the curb, breaking through a cemetery's metal fence and hitting a stone monument. By the time Kyd managed to untangle himself from the steering wheel, Irina was stumbling around the gravestones like a drunk. He chased after her, wheezing, grabbing her coat and bringing her down. Kyd crawled on top of her, pinning her arms beneath his knees. He struggled to regain his breath so he could speak. "I need the video disk."

Irina shouted back, "What for? Nicoli's dead!"

She was twisting and turning, trying to escape. He put his hand around her throat and gripped hard enough to get her attention. "It's my only way out. Where is it?" She stopped struggling and he loosened his grip. "Irina, you must know where it is."

She struggled to get up without success. "Why should I help you?" she asked.

It was true, the tables had turned. This whole adventure had started off with her needing him. Kyd got to his feet and looked down at her. "Because Nicoli wanted the evidence seen, and ..." He paused. "You trust me as much as your brother."

He offered his hand, but she stood on her own. He had an arm hugging his chest, wincing in pain. She looked him over, his face and clothes. He was a ragged version of the man she'd met on the train. "The video disk?" he asked again.

She wouldn't meet his eyes, defiant. "We didn't have it. We wanted you to get it."

Suddenly, it all made sense. Kyd shook his head in exhausted disbelief. Despite his pain, a cruel smile crept across his face. "Nicoli said I was good at digging. This is all a wild goose chase. You don't even know if it exists," he said, and pointed a finger in her face. "You put me through this! You brought me over here and risked my life for nothing. Do you really hate me that much?"

She avoided his question. "We know people who have seen it. It's in Grozny, a doctor has it." She was willing to make a concession. "I'll give you the information you need for finding him."

"Chechnya." Kyd knew about the bloody wars that were fought there. He knew of it as a Muslim frontier.

"That's where he lives," she told him. "He has it."

Raising his eyes to meet hers, he needed to know. "Why me? Why did you need me? There must have been others to choose from."

"I didn't think you were corrupted by politics or money. You never were."

He might have been flattered under other circumstances but wasn't sure how her explanation helped him. Looking at her, he came to a decision. "You're coming with me."

"No, it's only for you." She waved her hand in front of him, erasing the possibility.

"You can't stay here, Irina. They'll paint you as a traitor. They'll make you part of an underground conspiracy. Garin got rid of his opposition, and he doesn't need Nicoli's sister as a rallying point."

"No one will believe that," she insisted.

"It doesn't matter what people believe when you're dead. If this disk is real, it's all we have to bargain with. The Russians will want to destroy it and the Americans will want to show it. It's our only hope."

His logic was beginning to sink in. "An OMOH officer, a Major Zarefsky, knew I took you to the meeting."

"What did he look like?"

"Big, stocky, calm."

"A wound on his face?"

Surprised, she said, "Yes."

There was a new urgency in Kyd's voice. "I've met him. He's not someone who will give up. We have to go."

"What happens if there is no disk?" She looked away, hiding from the possibility.

It was the question he didn't want to answer. "How can we get to Grozny?"

Her daze cleared. "Not planes or trains. Buses would be the least guarded."

Kyd returned to the car and found Irina's pistol, noticing for the first time the small crowd of spectators assessing the damage.

Kyd grabbed Irina's arm above the elbow. "We have to go."

20

ZAREFSKY ACCEPTED THERE was more to his mission than he was meant to know, but he was a detective by nature. His instincts prodded him to find out why things were as they were. It was an itch that brought him praise in most cases. He had even stalked Sofia for a few days to see if there was someone else but came up empty. The major was still undecided about which was more painful—Did she need a better lover? Or did she leave him because she couldn't breathe the same air? With work, maybe knowledge could help him sidestep the land mines that threatened his career. He couldn't make himself believe Reynolds shot Petrov. Reynolds was in the wrong position, there was no weapon. And how would killing Petrov benefit the Americans? What was the information being traded and why? The puzzle pieces didn't fit, not yet.

Zarefsky entered the army's pathology lab, where a male orderly, wearing rubber boots and apron, washed blood down the drain. There were two naked bodies on exhibit, yet to be examined. Everything was dirty white. The pathologist, looking like an overripe kumquat, in her forties, ate her dinner on a clean autopsy table. Zarefsky had waited until after midnight to visit, knowing the rules were more easily bent when the higher-ups were asleep.

"Busy, I see." His charm needed exercise.

The pathologist glanced up at him and grunted in response. She showed no respect for Zarefsky's uniform or rank. He had no authority in the lab.

"I'd like to see the bullet that killed Nicoli Petrov."

The pathologist continued eating, cutting her steak with a scalpel. Zarefsky moved forward, sliding her plate down the table, out of reach.

She looked up at him and responded, "I wasn't told his death was being investigated."

Zarefsky held up his cell phone. "Perhaps you're not on the minister's quick-dial. If you would prefer speaking to him, I can arrange that. You may even get to hear what his disposition is like when his sleep is disturbed." She would be brave to call his bluff.

They spent a moment staring at each other, before the pathologist, with exaggerated effort, wiped her mouth and got up. Zarefsky followed her across the wet concrete floor to a locked cabinet. She opened a drawer with a key on her belt. "It can't leave this room." She pulled out a clear plastic phial with a small numerical label, the bullet rattled inside. She handed it to him. "A Russian tragedy," she felt obligated to say. She waddled back to her dinner. Tragedies were a treasured cultural commodity.

With his back turned to her, Zarefsky reached into his pocket and pulled out the shell casing he'd found at the CPA. Pouring the bullet out of the phial, he held it next to the casing. Both were from a VSS Vintorez, an army issued sniper's rifle. This further confirmed what he suspected—Reynolds's arrival, the meeting, and the murder had been staged. A political solution, and he was a dumb accomplice.

Zarefsky's phone rang. "Yes … Fifteen minutes." He pocketed the bullet and casing before he left.

Boris' wife, bent over, sat on the edge of the couch, using both hands to hold a glass of water. The glass gave them something to do. The children had been taken in by a neighbor. She didn't look up, as the coroner and his assistants zipped up the black body-length bag that held her husband and carried it out. The wooden stand still lay on its side, and the window's singed curtain sagged off its railing. A policeman holding a notepad stood next to the lieutenant patiently waiting.

Zarefsky entered from the apartment's hallway, having visited the kitchen. He'd seen the shattered vodka bottle and the knife had been packaged as evidence. Zarefsky took Reynolds's photo from the lieutenant and held it for the wife to see. "Is this the man who killed your husband?" His voice hard and impatient.

She didn't raise her eyes from her glass of quivering water.

"Look!" Zarefsky commanded. His voice startled the policeman beside her.

She focused on the photo. "There was another man."

Surprised, Zarefsky asked, "What other man?"

"He was older, bald."

"An older, bald man?" It was too much of a coincidence and lived outside the government story.

Zarefsky sat on the coffee table, his eyes level with the wife's. "There was no other man. It was the American," he insisted.

She looked down, avoiding his eyes. "My husband was a good person and a good father."

Zarefsky took the woman's chin and lifted it so she could only see his face. "Look at me." She did, like a small bird waiting to be crushed in his hands. "Obstruction of justice is a serious crime. Your children will be put in an orphanage. Is this what you want?"

He had her attention and tears welled in her eyes. "Think again. Didn't you see the American kill your husband?"

She gave a small nod. "Yes, it was the American."

Zarefsky stood and turned to the policeman. "Get her statement."

Walking down the steps of the apartment building, Zarefsky spoke quietly to his lieutenant. "There's a man guarding Irina Petrov. Use back channels, find out who he is. Keep it quiet."

21

THE US UNITED Nations' ambassador was to meet Clyde Sorrow on the National Mall, the Congressional Capitol at one end, the Lincoln Memorial at the other. Sorrow was seated on a bench outside the Smithsonian Natural History Museum. The Mall had been mostly cleared of snow and he watched the pigeons meander around hunting for food. Weren't they cold? Rather than fur or wool, maybe feathers were the answer. When he saw Madam Ambassador walking toward him, he stood to greet her. He knew her well enough to know she didn't drink or eat red meat. She'd once attended a tantric yoga retreat in Bali, and she gave money to the Free Tibet movement. A few of the little incidental things one filed away in his line of work. Before she'd reached her exalted position at the UN, she had spent some time at the Agency, so they had that in common. While he worked in Intelligence, she had worked in the Office of the Inspector General. Her friends called her Betty, he addressed her as Madam Ambassador. She addressed him as Deputy Director.

"It's too cold to sit, let's walk," she said. She led him toward the Lincoln Memorial. The pedestrian traffic was light, but steady. Congress was still deadlocked over the annual budget and the Smithsonians had shortened their days of operation until matters could be resolved.

Betty was straight to the point, he remembered that about her. "I was pushing on this Syrian thing based on what I was told." Her words came out as smoke signals. "Where's this evidence you promised?"

"We have an agent in Russia, but it may take a few days for him to be extracted." Sorrow sped up to her pace.

"He has the evidence?" she asked.

Sorrow was slow to answer. "We believe so."

She stopped to face him. "Belief is a wonderful thing, like faith, but religion isn't one of my weaknesses. When will you know? When will I see it?" Sorrow seemed to be considering, so she pressed forward. "Forty-eight hours? A week?" He didn't answer quickly enough. "Look me in the eye and tell me straight." She found his eyes. "I've got my pants around my ankles here, I promised evidence."

It was a sight he didn't want to imagine. Sorrow smiled. "Dancing lessons from God." He'd been waiting for an opportunity to use it.

Madam Ambassador took a step forward, only a breath away. "Fuck you." She turned and walked away.

As Sorrow watched her sturdy figure retreat, he pulled out his cell phone and dialed a familiar number. "Paul ..."

22

KYD AND IRINA arrived outside Moscow's Central Bus Station at first light. The sky was ice blue, and the air stung their noses. The station was long and wide with buses parked under the awning, side by side, like piglets at dinner. Cars, billowing exhaust, circled and stopped, dropping off passengers.

They had been walking for nearly four hours, skirting the main streets as much as possible, Kyd stopping occasionally to catch his breath. They didn't talk. Irina's silence felt like anger, but Kyd couldn't guess who or what she was angry at. Maybe she didn't know either. He was past that stage, and she would get past it too. Despite what had happened to her brother, Kyd suspected she still had hope her name would save her. If they were caught, she might claim she'd been kidnapped by a ruthless American spy. Maybe it would work, but he doubted it. They both knew of the government's allergy to loose ends.

Before they entered the terminal, he took her hand. She was surprised and tried to pull away, but he wouldn't let go. "The police don't know we're traveling together," he said. "They're not looking for a couple." She relented, reluctantly playing her part as the romantic companion.

Inside, they saw lines of adults and children waiting for tickets, many dragging wheeled suitcases and others hugging shopping bags stuffed with clothes or groceries. Buses weren't a first-class choice. The polished linoleum floors made the ramshackle travelers look like litter. Announcements for departures and arrivals bounced off the hard walls like gunshots ricocheting through a tunnel. Kyd and Irina kept their heads lowered, while yawning policemen sat on benches chatting, drinking coffee, or checking their phones. None of them dreamed of winning the lottery.

Irina's hand trembled in his and he pulled her to the side, behind a white tiled pillar. He spoke in a confident tone, as if she were still his student. "Take a deep breath, relax."

Her muffled response made it through the scarf covering her mouth. "This isn't a relaxing situation."

"I know, but we can do this," he said, a halftime coach trying to inspire a losing team. Still holding hands, hers was gripping his. "Just stay here," he told her. "I'll get our tickets. If something happens to me..." He looked around the terminal as if the answer was waiting to be found. "Use your best instincts." He couldn't think of any better advice.

"Be careful," she said, letting go. He tried out a smile.

Kyd made sure his scarf was up and knit cap down, exposing only his nose and eyes. Irina watched him make his way to the shortest line of waiting passengers. He didn't look back.

Her attention was caught by one of the TV monitors on the opposite wall. She was stunned to see her own face behind the muted newsreader. She moved closer to read the crawling subtitles at the bottom of the screen. ... *The Department of Internal Affairs is seeking Ms. Petrov for questioning. They will neither confirm nor deny that she is wanted in connection with her brother's brutal assassination ...* Then, Irina's face was replaced by Kyd's passport photo.

Kyd stepped up to the ticket counter. One of the TV screens was reflected in the teller's glass window. The newsreader's subtitles continued, ... *Douglas Reynolds, an American, is the chief suspect in the assassination of presidential candidate, Nicoli Petrov. Officials are asking the public's help in their search* ... Kyd pushed money through the slot at the bottom of the window, his scarf momentarily slipping down. He replaced it quickly, but the teller paused, looking at the face on TV, then at Kyd, recognition slowly dawning. The teller's face turned from open-mouthed astonishment to wide-eyed fear. Kyd took a step back, seeing his photo reflected in the glass, turned, and retreated at a steady pace.

Irina, petrified, was standing at the center of the terminal, when he took her arm, pulling her with him at a trot. "Walk fast, don't run."

Behind them, the teller pointed at Kyd's and Irina's departing figures, shouting, "It's the American spy! It's him!" The fugitives were weaving their way through the lines of travelers.

A young policeman, excited, jogged after them, while attempting to pull his pistol from his holster. He fumbled, screaming, "Police! Stop! Stop or I'll shoot!"

This got the attention of the other police and travelers. Screams and shouts started a slow-motion stampede. There was no telling which way was safe.

Kyd picked up the pace. "Run!" Their scarves fell away from their faces, running toward the exit, pushing in and out of the panicked passengers. The sound of the first shot echoed through the terminal, setting off a frantic scramble for cover.

Kyd and Irina escaped through the exit just before the second shot. He ran into the circling traffic, in front of a car with an elderly male driver, screeching to a halt. Kyd opened his car door, grabbed the driver by the arm and pulled him out. "I need your car."

The driver pleaded, "But you can't have it …"

Kyd turned for Irina, but she was gone. He pushed the driver aside, jumped in and closed the door, just as the young policeman with the gun ran out of the terminal. He spotted Kyd, as Kyd spotted Irina hiding between buses. Kyd drove beside her, door open. "Here!"

Irina was undecided until a bullet whizzed past her ear, hitting the bus. She jumped in the car and they sped away.

23

"ONCE I LEARNED his name, I found these in the military archive," the lieutenant told Zarefsky, proud of his ingenuity.

They were standing in the cemetery, Boris' crashed car and several police in the background. The black-and-white photo was of a soldier holding a rifle wrapped in ragged cloth camouflage. He stood in front of a building's rubble. Bodies could be seen strewn behind him. The soldier was smug and had one foot propped on a smoldering tank. He was bald even then. Zarefsky was examining the top photo in a small stack, as the lieutenant continued his explanation. "His name is Anton Tarkoff. He was a sniper in Afghanistan." Zarefsky turned to the next photo. Garin stood with several ministers, including Bortnik. Tarkoff was stationed behind them, looking over their shoulders.

Zarefsky flipped back to the photo of Afghanistan. "Can you identify the rifle?" he asked his lieutenant.

The lieutenant took the photo and looked at it more closely. "A VSS Vintorez."

Zarefsky had no trouble reaching a conclusion, but there was no advantage in it. He handed the photos back to the lieutenant. "No one knows you were looking?"

"No, sir. Back channels only."

"Good work," Zarefsky told him. "I want you to keep this between us, understood?"

A policeman ran up to Zarefsky. "Sir ..." He was excited by the news. "Reynolds and Irina Petrov were at Central Bus Station. They stole a car."

"They were together?"

"Yes, sir, they were buying tickets," the policeman replied.

"Where to?" Zarefsky asked.

"They were chased before they got one."

The lieutenant turned to the policeman. "Get the model and license number of the car. Make sure it's distributed."

Zarefsky spoke to himself. "Where would they go?"

24

THE CAR KYD had stolen was wedged between two others, outside Aviapark shopping mall. Kneeling on the ground, he tried to unscrew the license plate on the car next to his. Irina stood watch to warn of any approaching drivers. He only had a tire tool, and the flattened end was too thick to neatly fit the screw. Shoppers roamed the lot, returning to their cars.

"You should hurry," Irina encouraged.

"If you think you can do better, I'll move out of your way."

"Maybe it's better to steal another car," she suggested.

He was working hard to keep his agitation in check. "I don't know how to do that." He couldn't help questioning how he found himself on his knees in a Moscow car park listening to an ex-lover telling him to steal a car. "I'm just some idiot that got talked into doing something I knew would be a disaster from the beginning ... Fuck!" The tool slipped and Kyd banged his knuckles on the license plate. "This is hopeless." Kyd dropped the tire tool, staring at the ground in frustration.

Irina dug into her shoulder bag, fishing out a metal nail file. "Maybe this will work better."

He took it from her, biting back the obvious question. Within a few minutes, he had exchanged the plates.

Kyd drove, leaning against the door. If he could avoid potholes, his pain was almost bearable. Irina gave directions, she had a natural flair for it. She had offered to drive, but he figured the trip would take at least a day and both would need a turn at the wheel. He preferred to go first while he was most functional. They had managed their way out of the city using backstreets, only once passing a police car headed in the opposite direction. By sunset they were out of Moscow and traffic had thinned. Snow had been pushed to the sides of the road and he could see the small bright lights coming from houses where families ate dinner, watched TV, or had an evening drink. He thought of them as Good Honest Freds, people whose anonymity kept them safe. Irina, Nicoli and now Kyd made the mistake of standing out.

The heater wasn't working and their steamy breath fogged the windows. "You should have found a newer car," she said.

He thought she might be joking, which would have been a refreshing change of character. Kyd habitually checked the rear-view mirror for cops, aware danger could come from any direction at any time, and Irina had settled into a state of suspended anxiety, staring into the darkness. "I'm counting on you to know where we're going." Kyd looked at her and saw she was lost in thought.

She didn't look back. "What made you leave the CIA?"

One of the things he remembered about his companion was there were no innocent questions, everything was a clue to some hidden purpose. "The world needs more farmers." He glanced in her direction and could see she wasn't amused. It was a long trip and he could afford to elaborate. "I wanted to spend more time with my daughter."

"What is her name?"

"Molly."

"How old?" she asked.

"Eleven, last month."

"It must be hard for her without a mother," she observed.

"Life doesn't always give you what you want."

"And you don't have a woman in the closet?"

He looked at her but couldn't decipher her interest. Was this the best or the worst time for intimacy? He couldn't be sure. Kyd had had a fleeting affair or two using a dating website—shampooed hair, clean jeans, sports coat. Apart from his sparkling personality he didn't have much else to offer, and as far as datable women went, the pickings in rural Kansas were fairly limited. "My closet has muddy boots and old clothes." He could feel her eyes on him. "And what about you? You must have had some suitors?"

She dismissed the suggestion with a swipe of her hand and spoke to the window. "Yes, of course. They were unworthy." There wasn't a trace of humor.

"I'm not surprised." He was lucky to have known her before she'd raised the bar to impossible heights.

She switched to Arabic. "You were a good teacher."

He replied in Arabic. "I didn't like the students."

Irina switched back to English. "You liked one well enough." Was she fishing? Was an excruciating postmortem in the works?

"I guess the exception proves the rule," he said without conviction.

"I don't know what that means."

"Can't say I do either."

To Kyd's relief, she stopped staring at him and turned on the dome light, consulting a map she'd found in the glove box. "Turn left at the next crossing."

He was going too fast for the turn, and it was sharper than he expected. Twisting the wheel sent a sharp pain up his side.

She saw him wince. "How bad is your torso?"

He didn't answer, waiting for the pain to subside. She reached over and poked his side.

"Fuck! Shit! Why did you do that?" He was working to keep the car on the road.

She laughed. "I hope you don't talk like that in front of your daughter."

He was still wincing. "Christ!" He accelerated.

"There is a coal mine further south. It's closing down. There will be empty cabins, somewhere to rest."

"How do you know?" Kyd asked.

"I know. Nicoli and I went there, speaking to the miners."

"We don't have time." He was trying to find a sitting position that eased the pain.

Irina could see he was suffering. "You're no good like this. Pull to the side, I'll drive."

Kyd didn't answer, and she pointed a finger at his rib cage, threatening to poke him again.

"Okay! Keep your hands to yourself." He pulled to the side of the road.

25

BARNES HAD AGREED to meet a persistent old boyfriend for lunch, a few miles from Langley. She didn't mind the distance, she preferred it, it helped keep her personal and work lives separate. He was nice in the way nice is a turnoff. She preferred the guys who pushed back, the kind of guys that usually dumped her. Mulling this over, heading back to her parked car, she saw a familiar face. At first, she wasn't sure. It was a strange coincidence. Across the road, Wexler was strolling through a small park with a woman of similar age. They had stopped in the breezy sunlight. The woman was dressed neatly in a nondescript way, with no distinguishing features to remember. They stood close, facing one another. He was gesturing, angry or pleading, it was hard to tell, and the woman seemed unmoved, or maybe tolerant. Wexler never talked about his love life, and Barnes was surprised by his passion. He was different from what she knew, vulnerable. Neither Wexler nor his companion looked at home in the "wild," as if they'd been photoshopped into the landscape. Barnes' Russian wasn't perfect, but when the wind shifted, she thought she heard the woman speak the word *mertva—dead*. Barnes pulled out her phone and captured them in a photo.

Back at the office, Barnes attempted to use Langley's facial recognition software to identify the woman she'd seen with Wexler. Nothing came up.

26

KYD LEANED AGAINST the passenger door, eyes half-closed, unable to sleep. Molly would have had her first treatments the day before. If the operation was successful, everything he'd been through would have been worth it, even if he never saw the results.

The car slowed and he sat up to see a small constellation of lights rising in the distance, off to the left. "Is that it?" he asked.

"We can drive around on the outside," Irina answered. She drove slowly until she found an unmarked asphalt and dirt road heading toward the mine. The surface was broken into chunks, gouged out by dozers and heavy trucks. With every pothole, Kyd felt a sharp dagger of pain. He tried to sit light, using stiff arms as shock absorbers, but it wasn't much use. They skirted mountainous slag heaps, while the steady pounding and grinding of mining equipment rattled the car's windows. "Do you know where you're going?" Kyd asked as politely as he could.

"I need to remember," she said. Irina was concentrating, her chin over the steering wheel.

A large truck crossed a hundred yards in front of them. "Turn off your lights," Kyd told her.

Irina switched off the headlights, waiting for her eyes to adjust. The road led to a village of metal shipping containers materializing out of the darkness. They doubled as makeshift cabin accommodations, maybe a hundred. There was nothing orderly about how the boxes were placed. Some were bunched together, others looked like they'd been scattered by a centrifugal force. He guessed there had been many more when the mine was in full swing, but "housing" had been removed as operations wound down. Driving between the containers, Kyd saw ragged dark holes cut out of their sides, excuses for windows. The more sophisticated ones had clear plastic nailed over the openings.

"The mine has been shutting for two years," Irina told him. "Many should be empty." A few men could be seen, heavy silhouettes against floodlights, trudging to and from work. Irina drove to the outer perimeter, where the housing was scarce and spread wide apart.

Kyd pointed. "Park behind that one, it has a power line."

Irina parked behind the container, hiding the car, shutting off the engine. They waited for silence to take hold. "What if someone's there?" she whispered, even though they couldn't be heard outside the car.

Kyd took Irina's pistol from the glove box and put it in his coat pocket. "We'll tell them we're on holiday." Neither of them laughed.

They got out of the car, Irina walking closely behind Kyd. He kept his hand on the pistol, finger on the trigger. The metal box they'd chosen used concrete blocks at one end to level it. The corrugated iron door was ajar. Irina continued to look behind for any human movement, but saw none. The door creaked as Kyd opened it.

He entered, found a string hanging from an overhead light bulb and pulled it. The swinging yellow glow revealed a stained bare mattress on the floor and a milk crate next to a small wooden table—no clothes, no cutlery, and a small drift of litter against the wall. There was an old rat carcass and he booted it into the corner. The cold remains of a fire, toward the back of the container, had a hole above it as a chimney. Kyd closed the door behind Irina. He wasn't convinced it was any warmer inside than out; they could still see their breath. He wanted to be encouraging. "Doesn't look like we're disturbing anyone but the rats." Kyd walked to the mattress and kicked it as if checking a car's tire. He winced, clutching his side. "Shit!"

"Lift your shirt, let me see." She moved closer to him.

"Why, what can you do?"

"I volunteered in hospital," she replied with customary confidence.

He took a step back from her, not trusting what she might do next. "I've seen someone fly a plane, but it doesn't make me a pilot."

Irina moved a step closer and lifted her finger, threatening to poke him.

"You do that again and I'll kill you."

Undeterred, she moved within reach. "Don't be so much a baby, let me see."

After a moment's hesitation, he shrugged off his coat, letting it fall onto the mattress. He tried lifting his shirt but couldn't raise his arms high enough.

"Stay still." Irina pulled his shirt free of his trousers and unbuttoned it from the bottom. She was quick and precise. The elastic bandage Kyd had wrapped around himself earlier, had fallen in ribbons around his waist. "Lift your arms," she ordered. Kyd raised his arms tentatively, as if wading into cold water, but too slow for Irina. "Lift!" She pushed them higher.

"Jesus Christ!" It came out as a hiss between his teeth.

His pain amused her. "Now you've become religious. Come under the light, I need to see." Irina unwrapped the loose bandage and turned Kyd around to see his back. His rib cage was a deep purple.

"How bad?" he asked.

"Maybe you broke something. I will wrap again, tighter, until you see a doctor." She had high hopes.

"Take it easy, I don't want to be killed by a Girl Scout."

She corrected, "Hospital volunteer." Irina began wrapping the bandage high, above the bruise, pulling tighter, moving down.

"Fuck!" It helped to curse.

Her arms were around him. "You are not Russian. We are more tolerant with pain."

"Not bad at inflicting it either," he added.

She pulled the bandage tighter. Kyd gritted his teeth. Irina attached the butterfly clips, finishing. "That is the best I can do, Professor Kyd." She stepped back to admire her work. "Try," she commanded.

Kyd slowly lowered his arms. He bent a little to each side, testing Irina's work, and nodded approval. He certainly didn't want her to do more.

Her medical work finished, she sat down on the milk crate, satisfied. Irina watched him button his shirt. "You lie down, I'll keep watch."

He put on his coat. With nowhere else to sit, he gingerly corkscrewed onto the mattress. "If I fall asleep, wake me up in two hours."

"Lie down, it's okay," she reassured him.

Kyd lay back and looked at Irina's thin silhouette. Only hours before she was sister to Russia's next president—150 million people.

He closed his eyes and Irina studied him. She'd had time to take stock. "I would have come with you if you had asked. I waited for you to invite me." There was no longing in the comment, it was a soft rebuke.

He appeared to be asleep, and she looked out the dirty plastic window.

Finally, he answered. "It wasn't in our stars." He gazed up at the rusted ceiling.

"But the stars put us here?" she asked, turning back to him.

"I wanted to apologize, but you didn't respond."

"What for? You didn't want me, there was no need."

His answer came as a confession. "You were too young, or I was too old. Either way, it wasn't working for me. I was miserable and I would have made you miserable." He added, "I'm sorry I hurt you."

She didn't deny it. "As you say, it wasn't meant to be."

If she was opening up, he could round the corner as well. "My daughter's sick. The Agency offered to get her into a special program if I could bring back your video disk."

"Stem cells will help her. I see many good reports." Irina was looking out the window.

It took Kyd a moment to register what she'd said. "How did you know that? I never talked about her treatment." Irina was silent, but it was too late. Kyd sat up. "Who told you that?" Her back stiffened, bracing herself for his anger. "Wexler? You worked it out with Wexler?" Kyd was staring at her.

She was defiant. "He said you would come and your daughter would be helped. I'm not ashamed."

Kyd struggled to his feet. "You used my daughter to get me here?"

"And she will get the treatment she needs. What difference does it make?"

He turned back to her, his finger in her face. "The difference is you can't be trusted."

She stood, her words loud and sharp. "Would you come just for me? No, I don't think so. I know you love your daughter and I love my country. It's what Nicoli died for. If you don't trust me, I don't care."

■

The watchman, midthirties with a ragged beard, was stretched out on the seat of his truck, a half-empty bottle in his hand. He could park at the edge of the village, still in radio contact, but out of sight. His nights were long and routine.

The voices broke into his drowsy consciousness like a neighbor's complaint. At first, he wasn't sure he'd heard what he'd heard. A man and woman were arguing. The shouts floated on the breeze. Not even prostitutes visited the mine anymore, who had money? He stepped out of his truck quietly, leaving the door open to avoid noise, and walked softly toward the voices. They stopped.

■

Kyd had moved as far from Irina as the room would allow, as if he were avoiding contagion. The pieces were coming together. "Did you tell Wexler where I was meeting Nicoli?"

She didn't want to believe what Kyd was suggesting, what she had avoided thinking. It was too much. "He wanted to know if the location was safe. He works for the CIA," she emphasized.

Kyd turned on his cell and searched for a corner of the room where he could get reception.

"It's not my fault. You can't make me responsible," Irina said, her voice rising.

Kyd wasn't listening.

·

There it was again, the woman's voice. The watchman paused to light a cigarette, still not convinced he'd actually heard anything. It wouldn't be the first time he was fooled by an alcoholic dream, and he couldn't afford to lose his job over a drunken hallucination. As he approached, he saw a dim glow coming from the window in the last container. The watchman pulled a handwritten map from his back pocket and opened it to see the layout of the village. A red X marked each vacant accommodation. There shouldn't have been a light. He cautioned himself, it might be anybody, he needed to be careful. Moving closer, he saw shadows pass in front of the window. The man's voice was low, cold. They spoke in English. Then he saw the nose of a car poking out on the blind side of the container, it matched the description in the police bulletin. The watchman dared to believe he'd found the winning ticket. He used his radio to contact central security. It was hard to keep the excitement out of his voice. "I've found the American spy," he whispered.

27

OMOH Headquarters was a ten-story, semicircled structure on Marshala Vorobyova Street in Moscow. The buildings around it kept their distance, as if loitering too close made them suspects. Even though it was 7:30 on a Sunday evening, the lights on the ninth floor were shining brightly.

Zarefsky walked slow laps around the boardroom table, a table too large for Zarefsky's lieutenant sitting there on his own. He was reviewing hard-copy reports, looking for information he might have missed. The lieutenant put the ones he'd finished in a neat stack beside those still to be read. Beyond the table, there were computer screens staffed by six operators, each scrolling through maps, addresses and phone records. While no one spoke, there was the soft hum of activity. They'd been cloistered since morning, evidenced by overflowing ashtrays, rubbish from half-eaten meals and cold coffee. Zarefsky knew this was how it must be done, the monotonous, conscientious continuity of investigation.

The major spoke to no one in particular. "Dig into the past for friends of friends, anywhere they might go. They would be tired and need a place to rest." He stopped pacing when the lieutenant's cell phone buzzed.

"Yes?" He looked toward Zarefsky as he listened. After a moment he said, "You're certain?" The lieutenant hung up and smiled at the major. "They've been located on a mining site, off the M-4, near Boguchar."

The computer operators nearest the conversation stopped what they were doing, turning toward Zarefsky.

"How were they identified?" Zarefsky asked, having already received several false tips.

"The security guard recognized the car, and it was a man and woman speaking English."

That was enough. "Mobilize the police," Zarefsky ordered. "Tell them not to use their weapons unless absolutely necessary." He hoped to meet the American again, face to face. There would be a very different outcome.

■

Irina watched Kyd as he held his phone above his head. It buzzed and he answered. Kyd didn't speak first, just listened, then said, "The disk is in Grozny, we're on our way to get it now. Irina's with me ..."

Looking outside, Irina saw the small, brightened glow of a cigarette. She waved Kyd close, pointing out the window. He moved beside her, seeing the watchman's figure walking around their container. "The police are coming." He finished his call.

28

MINISTER BORTNIK SAT back, behind his polished mahogany desk. He had the phone to his ear. His heavy eyes gazed into the middle distance, easily ignoring the opulent setting he'd grown accustomed to. Everything was neatly arranged: books, family photos, even a large gold-framed portrait of his benefactor, President Garin.

"You're certain?" the minister asked, immediately remembering he'd never met an American who wasn't certain. There was a self-righteous arrogance he admired and detested at the same time. Still, the contact had been useful and his information accurate. He listened then responded. "How will you control him?" he asked. The minister knew whatever he was told couldn't be taken at face value. *Trust, but verify.* There would need to be safeguards. If plans could be trusted, they would have the camcorder's disk, and Reynolds, or whatever his name was, would have been eliminated.

"I have his daughter," Wexler reassured the minister. He had been passed through three channels before he was connected to Bortnik. The word *urgent* didn't seem to have the same meaning in Russian. Walking past an orderly in the clinic's corridor, he cupped a hand over the mouthpiece. The orderly smiled at him, Wexler was now a familiar face. Bortnik tortured him with a few more procedural questions before Wexler was able to finish the call. "Yes, of course, Minister."

Wexler pocketed his phone and entered Molly's room. She was lying in bed with bandages around her shaved head and seemed serene. Margaret stood beside her. To Wexler, Molly appeared more alert than before the operation. He didn't know if this was real progress or her hopeful nature. It seemed too soon for the treatment to be effective, but he wasn't a doctor.

Wexler's smile returned. "How is everyone?"

They had become used to his visits, he'd been attentive. Molly knew he had worked with her father, but there was something about him that didn't seem quite right. He showed you what you wanted to see, the "friendly Wexler."

"When's my dad coming home?" Molly asked, her voice clear.

Wexler hovered at the foot of her bed. "Pretty soon. He wants you to know he's working on something important but trying really hard to get back."

Molly knew the meaning of *patronizing*.

Margaret spoke up. "When we try to call him, it's blocked. Tell him to call us. He was supposed to be back by now."

"I'll try, but he may be out of range."

This reason satisfied no one.

29

KYD AND IRINA dodged between vacant containers, the watchman having stationed himself beside their car. Kyd reached into his coat pocket and found Irina's pistol, a useless last resort, but it somehow gave him comfort. He saw several cars approaching, their headlights reflecting off the mountains of debris—police cars. They were closing in.

Kyd told her, "We're better off separating."

"Look!" Irina spotted the watchman's truck, the door still open.

Kyd ran to it, Irina on his heels. He found the keys in the ignition, and before he could start the engine, Irina jumped in the passenger seat. He drove slowly with the lights off, watching the police circling their abandoned container.

The watchman walked back to where he'd left his truck. At first, he needed to convince himself he hadn't forgotten where he'd left it. There was a momentary pause, then he shouted, "They took my truck!"

Once on the main road, Kyd turned the lights on. The police cars soon appeared in the rear-view mirror, gaining, a school of sharks smelling blood.

"You have to stop! We can't get away! Stop!" Irina screamed first in Russian, then in English. Kyd knew she hadn't accepted what was waiting for her if she gave up. For all her accusations of corrupt government, she still had a sliver of faith in Russian justice.

With the police closing in and Irina screaming her head off, he pushed the truck as fast as it would go, which wasn't fast at all. The truck shook like a collection of parts. The police were on their bumper, red lights were flashing brightly, sirens were just a decibel below Irina's screaming. Then, as if in slow motion, their pursuers fell back.

Looking in the rear-view mirror, Kyd couldn't help but smile. So few of his strategies ever worked out, but this one did. "Looks like they got the message."

Irina looked behind and watched the police doing U-turns. She was amazed. "Why are they stopping?"

"They're following orders."

"What orders?"

"Wexler told them we were getting the disk. They need us."

"Why would he do that? He doesn't work for them."

"Money, politics, I don't know. It doesn't matter." He needed her to stay focused. "For now, let's just concentrate on staying alive."

Irina remained quiet, but he could read her thoughts. Kyd answered her unspoken question. "You couldn't have known."

She gazed out at the dark expanse in front of them.

30

Minister Bortnik stood in front of his liquor cabinet. The bright mirror behind the bottles reflected his face, which he could see resembled soft gray putty. There were several choices, but he was looking for a drink that complemented his state of mind. Normally, on a Sunday night, he would be having dinner with his wife, but the president had rung. He hadn't raised his voice or threatened but wanted to know what progress had been made. Bortnik knew from long experience it was never wise to disappoint the president. Concerns that might be expressed as casual interest could land you in Siberia or worse. Even though Nicoli had been eliminated as a political threat, Zarefsky had failed to capture the American and they still didn't have the evidence. But now, in a bizarre twist, it might only be the American who could get them what they wanted. Bortnik chose a bottle of Fernet-Branca, a medicinal, bitter drink.

When the minister looked toward the door, he wasn't surprised to see Zarefsky. He had been invited. "Ah, Major. Welcome." Bortnik greeted him with a smile.

Zarefsky found it hard to swallow his irritation. "The police were ordered to let the American go." He mentioned this as if it were news, although he'd been told the arrest had been called off at the minister's direction.

"Yes, that was my order," he admitted. "It became a practical matter." Bortnik lifted a short crystal glass. "Would you like a drink?"

Zarefsky tried to rein himself in. "No, sir. No, thank you." He watched Bortnik fill his glass. "May I ask why?"

"I forgot, your religion forbids alcohol." The minister took a sip and winced. "That's a shame, it can sometimes smooth the path to understanding."

"I believed my mission was to capture Reynolds."

Bortnik took his time, walking back to his desk, sitting behind it. "Your mission, as I recall, was to capture the American and to obtain the confidential material. It turns out Reynolds doesn't have what we're looking for, but he and Irina Petrov know where it is. Why not let them get it for us?" Bortnik waited for that suggestion to settle. "I haven't lost faith in you, Major."

Lost faith? Zarefsky needed to regroup. "May I ask where they are going?"

"I believe you know Grozny," the minister answered.

Zarefsky knew Grozny as home and as a battlefield. "Yes, sir." He needed to restore the minister's trust. He needed to get back on track. "How will I know this material?"

Bortnik leaned back, glass in hand. "You were stationed in Syria, were you not?"

The question caught Zarefsky off-guard. "I was an advisor."

"And you did an exemplary job, there were many complimentary reports." The minister tapped a file on his desk as proof. The anonymous file could have contained anything.

"I was only following orders," Zarefsky said.

"Bortnik's smile became tight, taking in the major's unease. "I don't think the War Crimes Tribunal will accept that excuse. They've heard it before."

"War Crimes Tribunal?" He'd been hit from behind. "Why would they bother me? I don't understand?"

"You helped the Syrian army target and launch missiles?" the minister asked, knowing the answer.

"I gave advice." Zarefsky's body instinctively knew what was coming before his brain did. A light sweat appeared on his brow.

Bortnik set down his drink and leaned over his desk. "You're being modest. Your expert advice was crucial to the success of the operation." Bortnik took a sip of his drink, wincing. "The missiles you helped guide carried the chemical agent sarin. It was very effective and the Syrians were happy for your help." Having made his point, Bortnik leaned back, allowing his words to land.

"But I wasn't responsible for what they carried. I did what I was told to do." Being defensive was an unfamiliar emotion for the major. He didn't like it.

Bortnik continued, "Reynolds and Irina Petrov will get a disk that recorded the aftermath of that attack. Apparently, there are Russians in the video. If the disk were exposed, it would challenge our diplomatic ability to explain our presence. As you know, we are against chemical warfare, we've signed an agreement." He saw Zarefsky had become very still, staring into the future. "Of course, we would do our best to protect you, but sometimes these things have a life of their own."

Now he understood his selection. "This is why you chose me." They hadn't selected him for his ability, they chose him because he could be controlled. He was vulnerable.

"You're a smart man, which is why you bring credit to your position." Bortnik paused, now it was time to offer hope. "Get the disk then take care of Reynolds and Petrov. Do this and everything can be resolved. As I mentioned, the president has taken a special interest in you." Zarefsky hadn't moved. "They should be arriving in Grozny tomorrow morning."

The president's interest no longer inspired optimism. "I'll leave now," Zarefsky said. As the major walked out, Bortnik tossed what was left of his drink in the waste bin beside his desk.

31

THE PINK MORNING light glistened in the dirty snow plowed to the sides of the road. As traffic into Grozny thickened, produce trucks, customized with colorful slogans, jockeyed for position. It was the argument of horns that jolted Kyd awake, bewildered. Irina had insisted on driving when she saw him struggling with his pain, disappointed her medical intervention hadn't had more of a beneficial effect. Kyd didn't put up much of a fight. Now, watching him stir, she asked the question that had been occupying her mind for two hundred miles. "What happens when we get the disk?"

Kyd had been dreaming about a woman he knew was Patty. Her face wasn't clear, but he knew it was her. They'd been walking along a deserted beach with waves of blowing sand. He was behind her, trying to catch up, but no matter how hard he tried, he couldn't do it. The dream made him feel empty.

He sat as straight as he could, clearing his head, wanting to give an honest answer, but he knew he was only confirming what she already knew. "We will have outlived our usefulness." Their journey was a bridge to somewhere and until they got to the end, there was still opportunity. It would present itself in an unpredictable way.

"They'll kill us?" It sounded like a question, but he knew it wasn't.

Kyd was thinking aloud. "We can't escape. They only turned back because they knew they could track us." He faced her and was satisfied to see she was no longer afraid. She'd finally crossed that threshold, the one he'd crossed two days earlier, when he'd emerged from the icy pond. Any time they had left was a bonus. They were numb to consequences, it was just a matter of moving in the direction they'd started. "If there is a disk, let's get it and figure the rest out later." For most of his life he'd been surprised by results he couldn't predict. He'd even learned to count on them. Kyd formed a view about fate, too, how it was the product of genetics and circumstance. If someone had asked a week earlier what the chances were he'd be sitting in a car with Irina Petrov, headed to Grozny, chased by the Russian government, he would have thought they were crazy, but here he was. He'd made decisions based on factors he couldn't control.

Kyd leaned over to check the gas gauge and saw they had over half a tank. "You stopped."

"I had to," she replied.

He nodded acceptance. Even when he wasn't part of it, the world kept turning. Kyd and Irina were silent as they entered the city's outskirts, each of them on their own mental adventure.

There was little evidence of the most recent bloody wars, when the Russian government twice put down the Muslim separatist movement. The wars had been going on for centuries, and Grozny was almost flattened by 1999. The rebuilt city was too new to have any character—clean, tall apartment blocks he'd seen all over the world. President Garin had installed a "mini-me" as governor of Chechnya, and the state was pretty much free of crime that wasn't federally sanctioned. He remembered the translation for *Grozny* was *cruel*. Something not likely to appear in the tourist brochures.

"Do you have directions?" Kyd asked.

"I need to call," Irina replied.

32

Wexler entered Langley's fitness center, where several employees fought with weights or thumped along on treadmills. He was sure, as he maneuvered around the machines and "athletes," Sorrow wanted to meet in the gym because he knew it made Wexler uncomfortable. In his customary tailored suit, Wexler could smell and feel the pungent, masochistic sweat. His trousers lost their crease. He located Sorrow jogging on a treadmill, facing a TV that played news with subtitles. He was dressed in shorts, runners and a sweat-soaked T-shirt, listening to something through earbuds. Wexler had to step between his boss and the TV before Sorrow noticed he was there. Sorrow hit the stop button and pulled out the earbuds.

Sorrow pointed a limp finger at the TV, showing scenes of destruction. "Things are going to hell in a handbasket." It was a safe observation.

"Good for business," Wexler commented, with only a trace of sarcasm.

Sorrow stepped off the machine. "POTUS is asking for an update. The White House called my office twice. That's practically a record. I suspect he's been chatting to Garin." Sorrow used sanitizing spray and a towel hanging from the handlebar to wipe down the equipment.

"We're almost there," Wexler said with confidence, wanting the meeting to finish as soon as possible.

"And where is that?"

"They've arrived in Grozny."

Sorrow was walking toward the locker room. Wexler hoped they could conclude their conversation before going in.

Sorrow made no attempt to lower his voice. "How certain are you the evidence exists? Maybe we've been chasing our tails."

Sorrow entered the locker room and Wexler was forced to follow. It wasn't as bad as he'd feared, but there was the sting of disinfectant in the air. He looked around at a few scattered men in various stages of undress. "Well, the Russians are worried, which is a positive sign. Kyd says it's in Grozny."

"Chechnya. And he knows how to get it?"

"Irina Petrov knows, presumably. They're together."

Sorrow found his locker. "Everything seems 'hopeful,' Paul. We're not good with 'hopeful,'" he said, channeling Madam Ambassador. Sorrow opened his locker door and took off his T-shirt. He used it to wipe his face and underarms, before tossing it inside. Wexler couldn't help admiring his trim, muscled body, usually hidden by a cheap suit.

Sorrow propped his feet on a bench, one by one, slipping off his shoes and socks. "We're under pressure to explain why Kyd's still running around. Our plan was for him to get the evidence and return. There shouldn't have been a ripple." Sorrow was taking off his shorts, but Wexler couldn't turn away without seeming prissy. Did Sorrow want him to look? His boss continued, now naked. "So, you've got an escaped assassin and the sister of the victim looking for a phantom video disk. Have I got that right?"

"We can pull him out now, if that's what you want." Wexler knew it wasn't, they were too invested.

"What happens if he finds it?" Sorrow asked.

"We'll get it out. We have assets." Wexler wasn't sure if any of this was true but continued. "They'll want it, we'll have it. Any other concerns will disappear."

Sorrow turned away, heading for the showers. "Get the disk Paul."

33

EVEN THOUGH IRINA avoided the main streets, Kyd saw a police prowler in the side mirror. It stayed behind another car, following a hundred yards back. And ahead, there was the nose of another police car poking out from an alley. They were coordinating by radio. For all Kyd knew, there could be hundreds of them ringing the city, lying in wait. "We're making friends," he told her.

Irina looked in the rear-view mirror and saw the prowler. "We should find where we're going." She found a place to park outside a row of shops.

Kyd rolled down his window and adjusted the side mirror. The prowler behind them pulled to the curb, staying at the same distance.

"Give me your phone, I left mine behind," Irina told him. Kyd fished in his coat pocket and handed it to her. She punched in the number.

"You memorized it?"

"The numbers spell 'big love.' That's how I remember." Kyd could hear a woman's faint voice on the other end. "This is Irina Petrov. I'm in Grozny." She listened, then said, "Yes, but we still want it. How do we find you?" Irina listened. "I'm with a friend ... I understand." Irina bent her head low to see a street sign and gave the address. She repeated the directions, looking at Kyd for encouragement. "Within an hour." Irina finished the call and returned Kyd's phone.

"That was his sister. She says she must speak to her brother. He'll be home soon, but she'll only meet with me."

"How far is it?" Kyd asked, glancing in the mirror again.

"Maybe three kilometers." They were quiet a moment, thinking about the inevitable precipice they'd reached. "We could get a train to Georgia," Irina suggested.

He knew she didn't believe it, but he answered anyway. "Everything is going to be watched."

She nodded, reluctantly agreeing.

Kyd noticed people carrying food, coming and going from a popular café bakery. There was a chalkboard outside advertising specials. "I need something to eat." Kyd pointed. "That place looks okay."

"What about the police?" She looked back at the prowler.

"They won't stop us before we get the disk," Kyd answered.

"They might think it's in here," she said.

"I'd rather die on a full stomach." He tried out a smile, with no reward. "It's better if you go in, you can use your scarf."

She looked out and saw some of the Muslim women wearing scarves that covered their faces. Irina arranged her scarf, wrapping it around her head, and looked in the mirror to see the result. Her eyes shone and her beauty didn't go unnoticed.

"Mystery suits you," Kyd said.

"The advantages of being a fugitive," she replied. She opened her door.

"Coffee, too, please." He pulled out the money he had left in his pocket and gave it to her. He watched Irina walk around the front of the truck, face covered, and enter the bakery. Kyd turned in his seat to see the prowler was leaving the curb and approaching slowly. As the police car passed, the two cops glanced in Kyd's direction but didn't stop.

34

THE FLIGHT HAD taken under three hours, but Zarefsky felt as though he'd been in the air all night. He'd been pushed into a corner, diminished by the people for whom he'd risked his life. Bortnik's not-so-veiled threat, the implied responsibility for a chemical attack he knew nothing about, hung around his neck like an albatross. He needed to still his compass, follow orders and get to the other side.

Zarefsky's small jet landed on a military air base near the city. There were a few hangars, but not much activity. As he descended the plane's stairs and made his way onto the tarmac, he was welcomed by the police chief, Sergi Barshev. The Ministry would have alerted him to Zarefsky's arrival. Barshev would have insisted on being there, for old times' sake. Zarefsky recognized Barshev's gold wolf's grin from thirty yards away. They were the same age, but Barshev was half Zarefsky's size. A few soldiers near the plane saluted, but the major ignored them. He took a direct path to Barshev, who stood in front of a black sedan with a driver waiting next to the open back door.

Barshev welcomed Zarefsky with open arms. "So, the prodigal son returns. *Assalamu Alaikum*, Alexi."

"*Wa alaykum asalaam*." The Muslim greeting slid from Zarefsky's mouth as an automatic reflex. He succumbed to a brief hug but parted quickly.

Barshev pointed to the jet. "It's not every day we are visited by such an esteemed government official."

Zarefsky and Barshev grew up together and both served in the Russian military. When Zarefsky leapfrogged Barshev to Moscow, Barshev took it personally. He believed, without evidence, that Zarefsky had reported his black-market activities to federal authorities. While this wasn't true, Zarefsky would have never supported Barshev's promotion. He was untrustworthy.

"Perhaps you'll have time to visit your mother while you are here?" Another sore point Barshev was only too happy to bring up.

"Are they in Grozny, Sergi?" There was no reason to say who "they" were. He wanted to keep the conversation within official borders.

Barshev took his time answering. "They arrived this morning. We have them under surveillance, but as instructed, we keep our distance until further ordered. The fugitives will not have much luck leaving Grozny. Not so much as leaving Moscow." Barshev grinned, letting Zarefsky know he'd heard of his failure.

Zarefsky moved to the back door of the sedan and got in. "I need to know who they meet, anyone and everyone."

Zarefsky started to close the door, but Barshev held it open. "A fortunate turn of events for our president. I understand Petrov had a good chance to win."

"Leave politics to the politicians," Zarefsky said, advice he was having trouble following himself.

If Barshev felt a sting he didn't show it. He took a step back. "Yes, of course, Major." Barshev gave Zarefsky a stiff salute, along with his golden grin, and Zarefsky closed the door.

35

KYD SAW THE police prowler that had passed by earlier, circle around and park behind, closer than before. The police had given up on stealth. If he and Irina were arrested before they got the video disk, they'd be tortured until the interrogators were told what they wanted to hear. The government wasn't going to this much trouble without getting a result. Pulling off fingernails or waterboarding wasn't the cleanest solution, but it worked as a plan B. From what Kyd knew, Russian interrogators weren't gifted with subtlety or patience. Kyd saw another police car park on a side street ahead of the truck. Two men got out. One was in a police uniform, the other he recognized as the bald assassin, his face still burnt red. They were approaching at a steady pace. When Kyd looked behind, he saw the two cops from the circling prowler marching forward. It wasn't hard to surmise that plan B had become plan A. Kyd took the pistol from the glove box and put it in his coat pocket. He stepped out of the truck and quickly entered the bakery.

It was crowded inside, with an additional entrance on the street behind. Kyd pushed his way through the waiting customers, searching, then saw her. Irina was standing at the counter. She had been handed a small cardboard box with two coffees and a brown bag with pastries. Kyd grabbed her arm, pulling her through the crowd toward the back door. "We have to get out, they're coming for us."

Tarkoff and three police entered. Tarkoff spotted Kyd and Irina at the same time Irina saw Tarkoff. She stopped, surprised to see a familiar face. Kyd yanked her toward the exit.

Once outside, they didn't know which way to run, their hesitation costing them precious time. Irina chose a direction. It was hard for Kyd to keep up, his chest was breaking. They ran down one lane, then turned into another, but Kyd had to stop, bending at the waist, gasping for air.

The shouts of the police were getting closer.

Irina scanned the street looking for anywhere they could hide. There was a row of parked cars and Irina, panicked, frantically tried the doors of each, all locked. Kyd hadn't moved. She then noticed an old Lada station wagon, beaten and abandoned in a rubbish-strewn vacant lot. She ran to it, pulled on the back hatch and it lifted. She shouted back to Kyd, "Here! Quick!" He wasn't moving, wheezing. She went back to get him, grabbing his hand and pulling him forward.

They climbed into the back of the wagon, Irina pulling down the lid and locking it. There wasn't much room, the back was filled with rubbish: a broken trolley, a bicycle wheel, and tattered bedding. It was a derelict's home. Kyd and Irina lay close, facing each other. She saw he was in pain and could hear his tortured breathing. She squeezed his hand for what comfort that might give. Kyd managed a half smile. If this was the end, he could think of worse ways to go.

The shouts from the police were louder and the red strobing light bounced off the Lada's filthy glass window. Kyd pulled an old, tattered blanket over them, then retook her hand.

Kyd spoke in a whisper. "You knew the bald man?"

She nodded. "Tarkoff. He was my bodyguard."

"He shot your brother."

Suddenly, a face appeared at the side window, trying to peer through the grime. They held their breaths as the back lid was pulled but couldn't be opened. Kyd slowly took the pistol from his coat, but the face was called away, and the voices outside faded.

Seeing the gun, she asked, "Would you use that?"

It was a question he'd asked himself. "If I had to."

"I don't believe you," she said. "You're not that person."

Kyd put the pistol back in his pocket.

Flashing lights passed by again and vanished. Kyd and Irina were silent. He could feel her breath on his face. "I'm still hungry," he said.

Irina surprised him by pulling out the brown bag from the bakery. He hadn't seen her carrying it. She was beaming. "Chudu, a Chechen specialty."

"And where's the coffee?" he asked, deadpan.

It took a second. Then she exploded into hysterical, crying laughter, and he put a hand over her mouth.

Kyd managed a deep breath. He understood the police would be working to cordon off the area. "We don't have much further to go." He knew their journey was coming to an end one way or another.

Irina let go of his hand, leaving him adrift. "I don't care anymore. Even if we get away, where do I go, what do I do? Will you take me to Kansas?" she asked.

"If that's what you want." Kyd couldn't imagine it. "You're doing this for Nicoli. He wanted to expose what they did."

"And you, why are you doing this?"

He had morals, but he wasn't a moralist. Unlike Irina, he had no philosophy about saving the world, it was too far gone in his opinion. He had his family, and that was it, that was all of it. "I want to get home."

It was late afternoon. They'd fallen asleep in the safety of each other's arms. He loved her and respected her as much as any person he'd known, without being *in* love with her, not like with Patty. Maybe that was enough. How would she cope in Kansas? Could she make a life there? Kyd stepped into sleep thinking about it.

36

THE GRINDING SOUND of the engine startled them awake. Kyd peered above the back seat to see an elderly woman, a colorful dropout, behind the wheel. He ducked back down. The station wagon had not been abandoned as they'd thought. It had never occurred to them it could be driven.

Irina was ready to get out, but he held her tight, whispering in her ear. "Let her drive us past the police, we'll jump out when she stops." She nodded agreement.

As the old car chugged through the city, police cars passed, their lights flashing the windows. Ten minutes later, when the wagon stopped at an intersection, Kyd pushed the back lid open, and they hopped out. They were shocked to find themselves opposite the central police station, a hive of activity. Kyd and Irina did their best to cover their faces with their hats and scarves, joining the stream of pedestrians on the footpath. They ducked into a busy shopping mall.

"We need to get directions," Kyd said.

Irina found an older shopper standing outside a clothing boutique. Kyd waited and watched as she spoke to the woman. The woman shook her head and Irina went on to ask a younger male shopper. Kyd watched as Irina received his directions, accompanied by hand gestures, as a cop brushed past. Kyd turned his back, browsing through a table of bargains.

Irina joined him. "The address is maybe two kilometers away. He said it was walking distance." She pointed. "I think that direction."

As police cruised the area, they hid, finding refuge behind sheds and parked cars, continuing when it seemed safe. Eventually, they entered a run-down residential area. The dogs were stirred up, barking at the strangers. Irina found the address. "This is it," she said.

"Are you sure? It doesn't look like the neighborhood where a doctor would live."

"You're not in America," she replied.

Kyd saw what looked like a gang of drunken teen thugs talking loudly, swaggering as they approached. He grabbed Irina's shoulders, wanting to make sure she was listening. "Don't go inside, talk to him at the door. If he has the disk, grab it and let's get out of here. We can make it work." He once more looked at the approaching gang getting louder and pointing out Kyd and Irina. Kyd was still holding her. "We're sitting ducks." He hoped that would translate.

Irina returned his gaze with a steadfast stare, reaching a conclusion. "If it's a choice between your daughter and me, it's right that you should choose your daughter." Before Kyd could figure out what she meant, Irina came forward and kissed him on the lips. She turned and walked toward the house.

The teen thugs confronted Kyd. The leader was holding a mostly empty bottle of vodka in one hand and a lead pipe in the other; his eyes were glassy. He moved close and grinned in Kyd's face. "Good day, my friend." He spoke Chechen.

Kyd responded in Russian. "What do you want?" He glanced at Irina, who was waiting at the door.

The thug followed the direction of his eyes. "She must be a nice piece of ass." His gang, equally drunk, chuckled. Their leader slapped the pipe against his thigh.

"You should move on," Kyd warned. When threatened, he found a place within himself that was steady.

"My mother's sick, I need money," the leader said.

Kyd pictured a mother hyena in her den, waiting for her cubs to return with bloody fangs. The other gang members circled Kyd.

"Sure, how much do you need?" Kyd asked in a friendly way.

The leader looked at his crew, then back at Kyd. "All you have." The others took a step forward.

"I'm happy to help a good son looking after his mother." Kyd dipped his hand into the pocket of his coat as if looking for a wallet and pulled out the pistol. He pressed the barrel hard into the leader's forehead. "Fuck off."

The leader continued to grin, turning to his gang. "He doesn't care about my mother." He threw the bottle he was holding down the road and it shattered on the pavement. Looking back at Kyd, he could see no weakness, and stepped around him. Kyd continued to point the pistol in the boy's direction, as his crew followed him down a deserted street. They began to sing.

When Kyd turned his attention back to the house, Irina was gone. "Damn it!" Kyd stuffed the pistol back in his pocket and headed for the front door.

He knocked and the doctor's sister, a stout, middle-aged woman wearing a housecoat, greeted him. She had the weathered lines of a tough life etched in her face. As she looked at him, there was the flicker of recognition. He could hear a TV in the background. Kyd looked behind her. "Where's Irina? She came for the disk. We're together."

"Your Russian is good." She knew he was American.

"Where is she?"

"She's using the bathroom." The sister looked him up and down. "You can come inside, someone might see you." She stepped aside, out of Kyd's way. Her home was dark, with over-stuffed furniture, curios, and family photographs.

"I've seen you on TV. You're the American spy." She wasn't frightened, more curious.

Kyd looked down the hallway, thinking he'd see Irina. "Is it here, the video disk?"

"That's my brother's business. After Nicoli was killed, we didn't think you'd come."

"Where is he, your brother?"

"He said you should wait."

Kyd moved around the woman, looking down the hallway again. Irina had been gone too long and he had a sinking feeling. "I'll just see if she's alright."

"Back there, on the right." She pointed.

The door was closed, and he knocked. "Irina?" There was no answer and opening the door, he saw the room was empty. He continued moving toward the back of the house, through the kitchen. The back door was still open. The small yard looked neat, with a little garden.

The doctor's sister stood behind him. "Would you like tea?"

37

IRINA WRAPPED HER scarf high, over her nose, attempting to catch a taxi. Several passed without slowing down. When police cars cruised past, she turned away. They would be looking for a couple, not a lone woman mingling in a crowd. What she wanted to do was dangerous, she knew, but no more dangerous than putting her life in Kyd's hands. He still had a whimsical ability to trust the unknown, as if he were guided by his personal angel. It was a philosophy better suited to an American than a Russian raised on Dostoevsky and Turgenev. Irina hadn't abandoned him. She'd held up her part of the bargain, leading him to the doctor. She only had herself now, no family in Kansas, or as Kyd sometimes called it, "The Land of Oz." A taxi pulled to a stop in front of her and she climbed into the back seat, careful not to reveal her face.

The taxi driver accepted her disguise. "I can turn the heater up if you're cold."

"I'm fine. Central Railway, please." If she could get to the border, there would be a way of getting across. She was sure of it.

The driver, in his sixties, wore a Muslim prayer hat and had a grizzled gray beard. His bulky sweater looked like something his wife made, too big for him with long arms. "Are you going for holiday?" he asked.

As much as she could, Irina tried to avoid his eyes. He needed to talk, so she answered. "Yes, out of the city." Then, Irina noticed a small picture of Nicoli on the driver's dashboard. A plastic flower was attached.

"I could use a holiday, but who can afford it," he lamented.

"I see you have a picture of Nicoli Petrov."

The driver immediately became defensive. "Anyone in favor of fair government would mourn his loss. He was a saint. What a tragedy for the Russian people."

His passion was genuine. Irina looked out through the window, suddenly accepting Kyd's fatalistic philosophy. Perhaps the driver, who stopped when others hadn't, was sent to help her. "How would you like to make enough money for your holiday, and to honor Nicoli Petrov?" she asked.

He was skeptical. "What are you saying?"

"I can tell you are a patriot," she said.

The driver scrutinized her with new interest. "What do you want?" He was suspicious.

"Drive me into Georgia." She was taking a desperate chance.

He was surprised. "That's a five-hour trip."

"I will pay you double your normal fare if you help me," she told him.

"Is it illegal?"

"Justice in this country is always illegal, but you will be safe," she answered.

He didn't know what to make of her, continuing to look in the rear-view mirror.

She lowered her scarf so he could recognize her. "Do you know me?" Her face had been broadcast all over Russia.

He swerved into the next lane as horns blared and he straightened his car. "It's you!" The driver stared, not quite believing.

"Will you take me?" she asked.

He gave this a moment's thought. "I will need petrol and cigarettes."

Irina smiled at her good fortune. "You can add it to the bill."

"Yes, alright. I will take you. You have nothing to worry about," he assured her. He soon pulled into a gas station. "I will only be a minute."

Irina pulled up her scarf as she watched him put the gas nozzle into his taxi, then walk into the store. She wondered if Kyd would have come with her if he'd known. Yes, maybe—probably. Once Irina arrived in Georgia, she could arrange an interview, giving some insight into her brother's assassination. She would do her best to clear Kyd of charges. The gas hose clicked off when the tank was full. Irina suddenly had an appetite, tension relaxed. She should have asked the driver to buy food for their trip. He was taking too long, and looking toward the store, she saw faces at the window looking back. Something was wrong.

Two police cars sped toward the taxi, blocking the exit. The policemen approached with guns raised.

"Get out of the car!" they shouted at her. She stepped out.

"Make sure it's her," one of them ordered.

The policeman closest pulled down her scarf, confirming her identity.

"I am Irina Petrov. Be careful what you do." She announced this proudly, with authority, but it made no difference.

Once she was handcuffed, the taxi driver approached. He spat at her, "Viper! Traitor! You killed a hero."

38

THE AKHMAD KADYROV Mosque in Grozny was unofficially referred to as "The Heart of Chechnya" and could accommodate as many as 10,000 worshipers. Zarefsky, in uniform, walked his mother to the entrance. He hadn't seen her for over a year and she appeared frailer than he remembered. His neglect wasn't from a lack of affection or respect, as much as avoiding her recriminations about his career choice. And of course, there was Sofia, the wife his mother had come to love. He hadn't seen the need to tell her about the impending divorce. His mother was a woman in her eighties. Did she really need more disappointment in her life? He held her above the elbow to steady her. Anyone watching would see a strange couple: the brute, and the wizened sparrow. Several of his mother's friends, seeing Zarefsky, moved away. They remembered the cruel wars and Zarefsky's allegiance to Russia. His mother had suffered trying to defend her only child.

The Call to Prayer was heard from blaring speakers placed in each of the four minarets. He knew there was no part of the city it wouldn't reach. Everywhere, the devout were performing their dutiful *wudhu*, the ritual washing of face, hands and feet, rolling out their prayer rugs.

His mother wasn't careful how she walked. Her right foot dragged over the smooth marble leading to the mosque's wide doors. "Sofia was a good wife, you weren't a good husband," his mother said in Chechen.

"She contacted you?" He had believed his wife, soon to be ex-wife, would have wanted a clean escape. Now he realized she needed absolution for her betrayal.

"She wanted me to know. You didn't tell me," said his mother.

"She was the one who left, not me."

"There are other ways of leaving. You left her alone. A woman needs a husband. Your father looked after me."

"She'll find someone more to her liking," was all he could think to say. He tried to keep the bitterness out of his voice but couldn't.

They had reached the entrance, and his mother paused outside. "Will you come in to pray?" She never gave up hope.

"I have work to do." He was already looking for an escape. Entering the mosque in a Russian uniform would make him a target and cause his mother further grief.

She raised her head and looked him in the eyes. "Allah knows what you're doing, my son." As the congregation passed, he could see they wanted to rescue his mother, when it was the major that needed rescuing.

"What am I doing?" He looked away, not wanting to hear the answer.

"You are a Muslim, Alexi."

"I'm Russian." This was precisely the reason he avoided her. Why did he feel guilty?

"They care nothing for you, they'll feed you to the dogs." She searched for his eyes.

Her prediction was more powerful because he was practically dogmeat already. His cell phone rang and he answered. "Yes?"

He turned to his mother, who had begun moving toward the entrance without him. A group of her friends had taken his place, helping her inside.

"I'm on my way," he said, finishing the call. His mother hadn't looked back.

39

IRINA'S FACE APPEARED on the TV. It was the same photo the media had used before, chin up, confident or defiant. It was hard to tell. The TV reporter was explaining recent developments. "Irina Petrov has been captured on the outskirts of Grozny. A suspected collaborator in her brother's assassination, she was discovered by Vladimir Dasha, a humble taxi driver." The image of Irina was replaced by an on-scene reporter, standing outside the gas station where Irina was arrested. The driver stood in front of his taxi with a microphone held in front of his face.

"Irina Petrov was a passenger in your taxi?" the reporter asked.

The driver straightened his prayer cap before answering. "Yes. She asked for the train station, then changed her mind and wanted me to take her to Georgia. I called the police."

"Did she say why she wanted to go to Georgia?" the reporter asked.

The driver looked at the reporter as if he were a fool. "Why do you think? She wanted to escape justice."

Kyd sat on the couch staring at the TV, then noticed the doctor's sister standing beside him. "I need to see your brother now, it can't wait."

As if on cue, the sister's phone rang and she answered. "Yes...
I will tell him." She hung up and turned to Kyd. "He'll meet you
outside the hospital."

Kyd tried to find a balance between being hidden and visible
enough to be seen by the doctor when he arrived. He stood on
the edge of shadow, near the hospital's emergency entrance.
Ambulances arrived with flashing lights and wailing sirens,
pushing the victims of disease and violence through swinging
doors. When the doors opened, Kyd was grateful for the
draft of tepid air. He hopped foot to foot to keep his blood
moving. He thought of Irina, what would happen to her. If she
told authorities how to get the disk, they may have reached a
compromise. Maybe she'd be forced to write a letter praising
President Garin as a great patriot. Anything was possible. He
could take her to Kansas, he'd decided, introduce her to Molly
and Margaret. They would treat her like an exotic star. Maybe
he and Irina would become lovers again, it was possible. Kyd
continued hopping up and down, his blood sluggish. After an
hour of waiting, he accepted the doctor might not come, but
couldn't think of anything else to do. He'd spent most of his life
waiting for one thing or another, disappointment was an old
friend.

A dark sedan crept past, and Kyd risked moving into the
open. The driver, a clean-shaven man in his fifties, slid down
the car's window. "Let me see your face," he said to Kyd. Kyd
was hiding behind his scarf. He lowered it and bent down. The
driver had a good look, then, satisfied, said, "Come with me."

Kyd got in the passenger side, his hand gripping the pistol
in his pocket as if it were a metal pacifier. The last rays of
sunlight were fading as they drove away. Kyd saw the driver
was nervous and took that as a positive sign. If he had the video

disk, there was plenty to be nervous about, even before transporting an American spy. How long had the doctor peeked out windows waiting for Petrov to arrive? How many times had he heard footsteps approaching from behind? How often had he questioned his decision to get involved in the first place?

The doctor looked over at Kyd, his voice unsteady. "I saw Ms. Petrov was arrested. Did you know her well?"

"No, not too well." There were too many things Kyd couldn't explain. There was only one thing that mattered now. "Where's the video disk?" How many times had he asked this question? He had come to think of the disk as mythological, like the holy grail. If the doctor had said it was all a gag, he could have accepted it, but he needed to know.

"I was only there to take samples. What was done was inhumane, terrible …"

Kyd interrupted, his anger impatient, a knife finding bone. "I need you to listen to me carefully. Are you listening?" Kyd took the pistol out of his pocket so the doctor could see it.

The doctor nodded. "Yes." His eyes darted in all directions.

Kyd made each word distinct. "I don't care about your politics, or what you did or didn't do. I need the disk." Kyd let that sink in. "Where is it?"

They were leaving Grozny, the lights dimming behind them. "It's with my cousin."

Finally, it became real. "How far?"

"Ninety minutes."

Kyd pointed the pistol at the doctor. "Let's get there quickly." The doctor nodded slightly, and Kyd could feel the car accelerate.

40

UNDER THE HARSH florescent lighting, not even layers of white paint could hide the prison's dark history. Mold grew in the corners, rust gilded the iron keyholes, and stubborn black heel marks on the chipped linoleum floor spoke of useless resistance. The prisoners were unseen behind steel doors. Chatter, shouts, and moans increased as inmates heard the passing footsteps of a visitor. Somehow, they knew the difference. Barshev was waiting for Zarefsky outside the last cell. This time there was no gold-gleaming welcome. Barshev was stone-faced, and seeing Zarefsky's aggressive figure approaching, he was prepared for the onslaught.

"Where is she?" Zarefsky's voice was a gunshot down the corridor's barrel.

Barshev took a step back. "She wouldn't talk."

"Where is she?" he asked again with dangerous grit in his voice.

There was no way to soften the blow. Barshev led Zarefsky to a cell door, it was unlocked because locking it was unnecessary—the prisoner wasn't leaving. Zarefsky opened it wide. The light from outside cut into the damp concrete cell. Irina was completely naked, unconscious, hanging by her wrists from the ceiling, her tortured, bloody toes lightly touched the floor—a tragic ballerina on pointe. Her head lolled to the side, face swollen, right eye black and closed. Zarefsky had seen brutality, especially in war, but this was sadism.

Zarefsky turned on Barshev, quiet but seething. "Is this your work?"

Before Barshev had a chance to answer, another voice was heard. "The Petrovs are tougher than expected."

Zarefsky turned to see Tarkoff, his face with a red sheen, a layer of skin gone. He buttoned up his shirt and dried his hands with a small towel.

Tarkoff met Zarefsky's angry stare. "I'll give her some time to recover, then start again."

"You did this?" Zarefsky fumed.

"The minister thought you might need help," Tarkoff replied calmly.

Hearing the minister had sanctioned the torture caused Zarefsky's stomach to turn. "She was leading us to the video disk!"

"She was leading nowhere. You should watch the news, Major. She was escaping to Georgia."

A policeman entered the corridor and Barshev went to meet him. They talked for a moment, then Barshev signaled to Zarefsky to join him.

Zarefsky turned back to Tarkoff. "Don't touch her until I get back. I'll speak to the minister."

Tarkoff only smiled, as if dismissing the demands of a rebellious schoolboy.

Waiting in Barshev's office, furnished with citations on the walls and a messy desk, a teenager sat between two policemen—the thug leader. Barshev looked down at the youth, the teen's sloppy grin evidence he'd spent the day drinking. "Stand up!" Barshev commanded.

When the thug was slow to respond, the beefy police on either side lifted him from his chair. He wobbled, training his grin on Zarefsky. "Nice uniform."

"He says he's seen the American," one of the policemen volunteered.

"How do you know it was him?" Zarefsky asked.

The thug tried focusing through a haze. "My mother has a TV."

Zarefsky continued, "Where did you see him?"

The teenager shifted his attention to Barshev. "This information must be worth something, no?"

The chief took a step forward and slapped the boy hard enough to rattle his teeth and split his lip. "You were asked a question."

Zarefsky asked again. "Where?"

■

Zarefsky paced outside the doctor's house, while Barshev interrogated the sister inside. He didn't need to be a witness, didn't want to be a witness. The doctor's sister had recognized him, she knew his mother. Zarefsky could hear her deny she had any brother at all, but after the sound of raised voices, pleading, muffled blows and sobbing, the house was quiet. In Russia, pain was always the cure. Urgency was important, he knew. If he could find the disk and arrest Reynolds, there was still a chance he could regain his reputation and the government's protection. This needed to be his purpose.

Barshev came out of the house. "She says he has a cousin in Itum-Kale. The disk you want is there."

Zarefsky knew this place. It was a village with steep mountain walls on either side.

"They left an hour ago." Barshev's gleam returned. "You'll need my help."

41

"HE EXPECTS US?" Kyd asked, becoming anxious.

The doctor drove down rough roads he knew well. "She'll be waiting," the doctor replied.

From what Kyd could see, the streets appeared haphazard, old stone buildings were mixed with houses newly constructed. Iron reinforcement bars rose out of their concrete, single stories, like porcupine quills, promising higher levels. The doctor parked but didn't get out of the car. He needed to tell Kyd something important first, something he'd been holding in. "I teach my son no matter what you believe some things are wrong. People need to know what happened, it was wrong. The evidence must be seen and the people who did this must be punished." The words weren't so much for Kyd, the doctor was giving himself a pep talk. It reminded Kyd of what Nicoli had said a moment before a bullet entered his skull.

Kyd put the pistol back in his pocket and followed the doctor to a small building. The streets were mostly empty and quiet, he heard a TV. The doctor knocked on the door, and after a moment, a plump woman in her forties answered. There were the sounds of children in the background, and the smell of a freshly cooked dinner. She looked Kyd over, no doubt comparing him to the photo she'd seen.

"This is the American," the doctor introduced.

"Yes," she said, accepting it was true.

She was holding a letter-sized white envelope. "Is that it?" Kyd asked the woman. It seemed too small, for all the importance it had been given.

Low at first, the trembling rumble of a helicopter was approaching. Kyd looked behind him and saw the lights coming over the ridge. The searchlight felt its way over the village like an insect's antenna.

"You promised!" she shouted at the doctor. He had told her she had nothing to worry about.

The doctor's cousin quickly retreated inside with the envelope, closing the door. As the helicopter hovered above, the searchlight found Kyd and the doctor. The doctor looked up into the light, blinded, then ran. There was a sudden burst of machine-gun fire and the doctor fell to the ground, his legs destroyed. Kyd kicked open the door and entered.

Zarefsky sat beside the pilot. "Cease fire!" he shouted. Several soldiers and an army machine-gunner stood. "I want him alive!" The major pictured himself in a newspaper photo standing beside the handcuffed spy.

Landing, the soldiers jumped out, running under the helicopter's blades.

Kyd stormed through the house in a frenzy, running past the two crying children. He found the doctor's cousin cringing in a corner of her bedroom, beside a bedridden elderly man.

"Don't hurt me," she whimpered.

Kyd could hear the soldiers rampaging through the house, and the children's cries go from alarm to hysteria.

"Where is it?" Kyd shouted, pulling out his pistol and pointing it at her. It wasn't necessary. She held the envelope out to him as if it were burning her hands. He grabbed it, pocketing his pistol. He didn't have time to look inside the envelope, the soldiers were only steps behind. He opened the window and climbed out just as the soldiers entered the room.

Kyd ran through the maze of streets, searching for any route that might offer him an escape, but his luck had run out. He was met by a newly constructed dead end. Kyd stuffed the envelope in his coat pocket next to the pistol and prepared to scale the wall. He needed to catch his breath first, his ribs were screaming.

There was a strong even voice behind him, a voice he recognized. Zarefsky spoke English. "You must stop now."

Kyd took one more step toward the wall, when a bullet shattered the bricks above his head. "The next one will be in your spine." The voice was that of a winner, even casual, a good sport's declaration, usually followed by a friendly handshake.

Kyd raised his arms as far as he could, and turned, facing Zarefsky for the second time. Kyd could see the circular wound in his cheek was still fresh. Zarefsky pointed his revolver at Kyd's head, approached, and held out his unarmed hand, palm up. Words, English or Russian, were unnecessary. Kyd dipped his hand into his pocket, felt the pistol and pulled out the envelope, giving it to Zarefsky. The major tore it open, looked inside, and found the small camcorder disk. He turned it over in his hand, as if searching for something more significant.

"I have a pistol in my pocket," Kyd offered. "The left one." He thought a generous surrender might weigh in his favor.

The major considered and took a step forward, retrieving Kyd's weapon. Looking Kyd in the eye, Zarefsky said, "Your vacation is over, Mr. Reynolds." No trace of a victor's smile.

Zarefsky entered the empty police office and closed the door. He had asked for a computer to be fitted with an auxiliary device so he could access the evidence. Given the trouble he'd gone to in getting it, he felt he had earned the right to view it. Sitting in front of the screen, he found the port, installed the disk, and hit play.

42

DALAL WAS HANGING out in her family's electronics store. There was no school and her father had stopped answering her questions about the nature of the universe. Bored, she began rummaging through shelves of discarded equipment in the back room, where she discovered an old, beaten-up camcorder. Her father didn't care, he was happy to be left alone. The video camcorder came to life once she'd found the right wire, in a rat's nest of wires, to charge the battery. It took most of the day, checking on it every couple of hours. Electricity was undependable.

Even though Dalal had walked down Al-Bahrah Street hundreds of times, the camera's viewfinder made her small town look glamorous. Mothers carrying bags of shopping, dusty boys kicking a football, even the knots of grizzled old men squatting on the street corner, sipping little cups of coffee—they could all be movie stars.

Dalal wandered through the market pointing her camera in every direction until she stopped outside a small greengrocer's stall. He was squeezed between a makeshift pharmacy and a nut specialist. The gray-bearded grocer polished an apple on his stained white kaftan. When the apple gleamed he placed it in a display box among other apples, as though they were diamonds in a jeweler's tray. He stood back admiring his collection, slightly readjusting one or two pieces of fruit to hide any spots.

"Speak to me," Dalal demanded, training her camera on his face.

Malmoud was something of a family friend, he had supplied her family with fruit and vegetables since the beginning of time. His sad thin dog, Alfie, sniffed the ground at Dalal's sandalled feet, looking up at her, expectant, wagging his tail. She recorded the dog's crooked grin as evidence that owners do look like their pets.

"What are you doing with that?" Malmoud got the camera's attention.

"Make a face," she directed.

Malmoud made the face of a gargoyle, using two fingers to pull down his eyes and another to push up his nose.

Laughing, she warned, "Be careful, it might freeze."

"Not in this weather." Malmoud began stacking the oranges. "Your mother must be close, eh?"

Dalal's mother was expecting her fourth child, everyone hoped it would be the first boy. The grocer chose another orange from a box below the table, rubbing it clean on his kaftan.

"I will ask her to film the birth." Dalal took a fat date from the table, popped it in her mouth and spat out the pip. "I know where babies come from," she said, as if he might doubt her biological knowledge.

"Your mother doesn't need to be disturbed by a silly daughter." He looked into the camera. "So, you want to make movies?"

"Yes, why not?"

"Yes, why not? I can be your star."

"A horror movie," she said, smiling.

They were distracted by honking horns and cheerful shouts. A ragtag group of rebels was walking down the street. They ranged in age from teenagers to men with gray beards. The rebels stopped at stalls to grab whatever caught their eye, escorted and circled by coughing motorcycles belching smoke. Dalal turned her camera in their direction, the viewfinder framing their tired faces. They dressed in a mixture of salvaged army uniforms and personal clothing, each of them carrying a battered assault rifle. The rifles seemed more like required baggage than weapons. One of the older rebels balanced a young child on his shoulders.

Through her camera, Dalal discovered Omar, not a whisker in sight. When he saw Dalal, he left the others, chin up, and swaggered toward her, a red Metallica T-shirt peeked out from an oversized army jacket. Omar wasn't confused by Syrian politics; his father had been killed by government forces in a town flattened by artillery. That was all he needed to know.

"Revolution until liberation!" he chanted. Omar was sixteen.

"Make a mean face." Dalal directed. She brought the camera closer, so that Omar's head filled the frame. He tried to do what she asked, but his smile won out.

"My hero," she teased.

"Where'd you get that?" He moved out of frame, self-conscious.

Her camera followed him. "Found it."

Omar took the camera and turned it on Dalal. A faded blue scarf made an oval of her dark face. She smoothed her luxurious black eyebrows, striking a model's pose. "Am I pretty?"

"I've seen better," he said.

She punched his shoulder and took back her camera.

"No brother yet?" It seemed the whole town knew of the impending birth. Omar looked down the road at his rebel group. They continued through town like a small herd of cattle, grazing, scuffing the dust.

"Maybe today," she told him.

Omar selected one of Malmoud's apples, leaving a hole in the display, and took a crunchy bite. Malmoud was ready to complain, when there were two muffled explosions just outside of town, two puffs of smoke, missile strikes. Street life ducked, some running for cover, others frozen like statues, heads swiveling like radar dishes, predicting more. No one knew what might happen next. The government had declared Dalal's town a "rebel village" after the local mayor had been kidnapped and executed as a collaborator. No one was sure whom he had collaborated with.

Dalal raised her camera, recording the thinning smoke caught in a gust.

"Government marksmanship!" Malmoud announced with ironic humor.

Townspeople began moving again, but more quickly and warily, as if preparing for an unseen invasion. The rebels who had scattered, regrouped in a tight unit.

"I'll protect you," Omar reassured Dalal, and the viewfinder found his brave face. Dalal had always thought that someday she and Omar would marry. He would keep her safe.

Alfie, Malmoud's scruffy dog, whimpered, then began doing a comical dance as if the ground were too hot for his paws. Omar chuckled and the animal looked up at Dalal before it collapsed in convulsions. She raised her camera and saw shoppers, storekeepers and crying children coughing, staggering, as if suddenly drunk. She pointed the camera at Omar, hoping he had the answer, but he looked astonished, wide-eyed, his face twitching. Listing, his right leg buckled before his left and he fell over, his body jerking uncontrollably, slobber spilling from his mouth in frothy ropes. The camera dropped from her hands, and as the small red recording light blinked, all street life faltered.

Malmoud tumbled over his display and an orange rolled toward Dalal's lifeless body.

·

A platoon of uniformed Syrian soldiers, rag-masks protecting their noses and mouths, dragged the dead bodies into rows side by side. At first, they had tried to guess which family members belonged together, but not all the victims died immediately. Some staggered yards from the others. It was decided all the children should be buried together, men together, and women together. It was the respectful thing to do.

Six inspectors, wearing white biohazard suits, visited the scattered victims to take biological specimens. Two of the inspectors grew in Dalal's viewfinder, carrying medical kits, kneeling beside the bodies. The sun's glare off their visors distorted their faces, a woman and a man. While the woman used a swab to take a sample from Omar's mouth, the man paused to look at Dalal, her scarf bunched around her head, revealing thick black hair.

"How old do you think they are?" The male inspector spoke Russian.

"Maybe fifteen, sixteen." The woman continued the business of slipping her used swabs into test tubes, storing them in an open container labelled in Cyrillic.

"They're my son's age." The male inspector turned to watch the soldiers stack the bodies on carts. It reminded him of the pictures he'd seen of the Holocaust. "They were unlucky with the wind."

"Allah be praised." Her voice was tired, remote.

Working with the Syrian government had been difficult. The Russian inspectors had been forced to wait three days in a cheap Damascus hotel before the attack. The food was bland and the beds lumpy.

Picking up Dalal's camcorder, the male inspector saw the recording light blinking red. He found the switch and turned it off, his head angled in a way that made his face visible—a middle-aged doctor with a furrowed brow. His female partner closed her case and stood, looking back down the street at the other inspectors boarding a white van.

"Let's get out of this shithole, we have a flight to catch." She walked away to join the others.

The male inspector covered Dalal's face with her scarf.

43

ZAREFSKY REWOUND THE video to the missile strikes. The young woman spoke Arabic, but he had no trouble understanding. Her innocent enthusiasm made up for any technical problems. She was a young Muslim woman, blossoming. Missile strikes, puffs of smoke outside town, the dog collapsing, the boy tilted then falling into jerking convulsions. He heard the young woman's frightened voice calling the boy's name. Villagers staggered in the background, like comic marionettes whose strings were cut one at a time. The camera fell but continued to record. Zarefsky moved forward in this seat and advanced the tape, past the streaking stillness until two inspectors approached the camera. They both spoke Russian and Zarefsky recognized the doctor. The major sat quietly, absorbing what the disk meant to him and his career, when he heard the female inspector say, "Allah be praised." He replayed the mocking comment and it bothered him in a way he couldn't have predicted. It was as if he'd been walking on water and suddenly looked down.

He rang Barshev. "It's Zarefsky. If I need transport to Tbilisi, can you arrange that?" He listened. "A helicopter with no record of the flight." Barshev would make assumptions. "Holidays never do anyone any harm," Zarefsky told him, attempting to keep the request light. "*Salaam alaikum.*"

"Are you ready?" It was Tarkoff waiting in the doorway.

■

The holding cell was dark except for a thin, flattened, horizontal slit of light squeezing beneath the door. Kyd had a first-class view of this, hanging by his feet, his hands cuffed. At first, he counted himself lucky, believing his ribs couldn't have handled being strung up by his wrists, but after three hours, so he imagined, it didn't make much difference. He saw himself as an old-fashioned thermometer, his head throbbing red at the bottom. Kyd's face had taken a beating for no particular reason, being asked questions without answers. Granted, he'd given them a hard time, something he remained proud of, and they wanted their pound of flesh, but in the end whatever they did to him was pointless and displayed a lack of human compassion. Kyd would let them know before they killed him.

Kyd's cell was larger than a normal jail cell and had slimy puddles on a dirt floor. It reminded him of a country slaughterhouse. He saw movement around the walls and assumed it was hungry rats waiting for the dinner bell. His body swayed, as if pushed by a gentle breeze, but there was no breeze. He was moved by the rhythmic beat of his heart and his wheezing lungs. Kyd wondered if he and Irina were swinging in rhythm.

First the rough footsteps, then an explosion of light. Kyd could see two male figures approaching in silhouette. The door was pushed shut and an overhead light came on. Tarkoff, the bald assassin, approached, and Zarefsky stood a few steps behind.

Tarkoff leaned down, his face close. "You must be tired of waiting. Maybe you thought your government would save you. They don't care about you. You're a problem for them."

Probably true. Seeing Tarkoff's freshly scarred face, and understanding nothing he could say could make matters worse, Kyd asked in his best Muscovite accent, "Does it hurt when you smile?"

Tarkoff proved he could smile, punching Kyd in the ribs. Kyd screamed in pain, emptying his lungs. Perhaps matters could get worse. Tarkoff opened a folding knife he took from his pocket. It was a sharp upgrade from the one he'd left behind in Boris' kitchen. Zarefsky remained in the background, content being a silent witness.

Kyd looked at Zarefsky's swaying figure and struggled to gather breath. "He's the assassin ... He killed Petrov." Kyd wasn't sure why he bothered. Was he still searching for Russian justice?

Tarkoff punched Kyd again, enjoying himself. "He still talks." Tarkoff turned to Zarefsky, wanting to share his enjoyment.

Zarefsky spoke in the even, measured, dangerous tone Kyd recognized. "Why would he kill Petrov before he received the video disk."

Tarkoff looked at Zarefsky quizzically, then with amusement, as if the joke had just landed. "This is not a trial, Major. I'll put in a good word for you. Maybe with a promotion you can get your wife back."

Kyd swung like a pendulum, still propelled by Tarkoff's last punch.

"You have a VSS rifle. I saw it in a photograph. You left the shell at the CPA," Zarefsky told him.

Tarkoff was unconcerned. "We all follow orders. You can always discuss matters with the minister if you wish."

Kyd once more gathered his breath, speaking in Arabic. "Be just; that is nearer to righteousness. And fear God; indeed, God is acquainted with what you do."

Tarkoff was impressed, as if watching a dog walk on hind legs. "What's he saying?"

"He's quoting the Qur'an." Zarefsky knew.

Kyd fought to stay conscious, the upside-down men ignoring him.

Tarkoff nodded. "Maybe he's one of yours." He stopped Kyd's wayward motion, the knife's point aimed at Kyd's gut. Tarkoff was practically salivating. "I will now show you something you've never seen before and will never see again." Kyd knew the rats were ready.

"Move away. You're under arrest for the murder of Nicoli Petrov."

Tarkoff laughed, moving in with his knife.

The pistol's blast and the blood that splattered Kyd's face brought him back to life. Zarefsky holstered his gun and moved to the winch. Releasing the lever, Kyd fell in a heap.

Zarefsky pulled the white envelope from his pocket, bent down and slapped Kyd's face to get his eyes open. "What will you do with this?"

Kyd swallowed hard. "Show it." He was past caring.

There was a moment of silence before Zarefsky's cell phone rang. He looked at the caller's name and answered. "The disk has been destroyed ... Reynolds is dead ... Of course, Minister. Thank you." Zarefsky ended the call and stuffed the envelope into Kyd's pants' pocket. He uncuffed Kyd's hands and stood. "There's a car waiting."

Kyd spoke into the dirt as Zarefsky opened the door. "What about Irina?"

Zarefsky didn't turn around. "Don't come back to Russia." He vanished into the light.

It took Kyd a couple of minutes to straighten his body and gather his thoughts. He knew he had to move before the major changed his mind, but his body didn't follow his commands. It wasn't until he turned his head and saw Tarkoff's empty eyes immediately in front of him that he mustered the energy to stand.

Once outside in the sunshine, he looked for guards and there were none. An open gate beckoned, with a waiting car and a policeman standing beside it, smoking. As Kyd stumbled forward, he paused outside the open cell next to his. Looking inside he saw a dead woman, naked, curled on the hard dirt floor, eyes open and blank, surrounded by rats. Irina had taken flight.

"Here!" the policeman yelled, impatient. Kyd leaned forward, letting gravity lead him out.

44

ZAREFSKY, DRESSED SIMPLY in a white kaftan, prayed with another hundred worshipers. His prayers, combined with theirs, resonated beneath a vast and ornate domed ceiling. No one recognized him out of uniform. At first, he felt awkward, an imposter, but as the remembered ritual took hold, there was peace, more than he'd felt in years. He'd found home, around which other things could find their rightful place. It was as if a hidden longing had been satisfied. He'd been an honored warrior for the Russians, but now, in this holy sanctuary, surrounded by other devout Muslims, his presence was unexceptional. He was accepted as a drop of water in the ocean. Whatever would surely happen to him in the following days couldn't erase who he was at his core, who he'd always been. His mother would be proud.

As the service finished, Zarefsky turned and saw his faithful lieutenant standing with Barshev and two OMOH soldiers near the entrance. They wouldn't enter the holy sanctuary, so Zarefsky went to meet them, calm in his heart.

45

EVERYTHING HAPPENED QUICKLY, more quickly than Kyd thought possible or could have predicted. A waiting helicopter flew him to an air base in Georgia, near Tbilisi, where a military doctor did a proper job of strapping his chest and gave him drugs to ease the pain.

He rang Margaret. "It's me. How's Molly?"

"She's fine. When are you coming home?"

"As soon as I can." He could hear Molly in the background asking for the phone.

His daughter's voice was stronger than he remembered. "Where are you?"

"In Tbilisi, Georgia." He knew she was already googling it.

"Are you alright?" she asked him, turning the tables.

He put on a cheery voice, as if he'd just golfed under par. "Right as rain. I'll be home soon."

"Did you finish your work?"

"All done."

Margaret was back on the line. "An Agent Barnes was here. She wants you to call on her private number. She made it seem important."

"Okay, thanks. What's her number?"

After he'd hung up, he dialed Barnes. Agents didn't normally give out their private numbers. She answered on the third ring. "It's Kyd."

"Where are you?" He could hear an urgency in her voice, she was pulling out a notepad and pen.

"Why do you want to know?"

"I can bring you in. Do you have the disk?"

The fucking disk! What about his life? "Yes, I have it."

"Bring it to Langley and I can protect you." When he didn't answer quickly enough, she added, "I can arrange everything."

"What happened to Wexler?"

There was a long pause. "He may be unreliable."

"That's another way of putting it."

"Get the disk here and I'll take care of everything else."

"I'm in Tbilisi. I don't have a passport," he told her.

"Ring me back in ten minutes," she told him, and hung up.

■

Wexler was in his office when he received the news Kyd was dead. Apparently, Kyd had been outsmarted by a dedicated and resourceful security force. The Russian news media had described his death in custody as suicide, a common occurrence. Wexler had to admit Kyd had displayed exemplary survival skills, more than anyone would have predicted. How had the linguist found another gear? Wexler felt satisfied Kyd had traded his life for Molly's. She was a remarkable child, Patty's kid, struggling with the hand she'd been dealt. Wexler had kept his part of the bargain, and he felt virtuous about that, taking credit for her improvement. Perhaps, at some stage, he could become something of a surrogate father. It might fit him like a well-tailored suit. *She's not my daughter, exactly*, he would say.

Then an aside, *Her mother and father were dear friends*. Molly would need a male influence in her life—discussions about school, fashion, boys. Wexler's daydream was becoming nicely rounded when his phone broke the spell. Kyd had been spotted, resurrected, on security footage at DC's Dulles Airport.

46

WHEN KYD ARRIVED in DC, he decided showing up at Langley was a bad idea. Who could he trust? Barnes? Certainly not Wexler. There was a three-hour direct flight to Kansas City.

Kansas snow was different from Russian snow. It appeared lighter and brighter, but it might have had to do with getting closer to home. Kyd was ragged exhausted with a few days' beard camouflaging his battered face. He felt like he hadn't slept since leaving Margaret's. He rented a car in Kansas City, and had been driving for two hours, leaning against the door. Kyd resisted taking the last of the drugs he'd been given in Georgia, he needed to be alert for what would certainly come next. There was plenty of time to think, swirling images, but the memory of Irina curled on the dirt floor left an impression he would never forget. What had they done to her? It had flipped a switch somewhere deep inside him. He was no longer the person he'd been a week before. He wanted to hurt someone, someone had to pay. Kyd glanced at the passenger seat beside him and saw the tattered white envelope Zarefsky had tucked into his pocket, the reason for all of it.

The clinic was in Wichita. Kyd had been there once before to get Molly examined. He parked in front of the entrance, and on second thought, took the last two painkillers before walking in. If something needed to be killed, why not pain first?

At the neat, gleaming reception desk, he approached the uniformed nurse on duty. Her delicate perfume was the antidote to how he felt. "I'm looking for Molly Kyd." He did his best to be friendly, but his impatient manic voice worked against him.

She took in his deep-set eyes and haggard face. "Are you a relative?"

He looked down the corridor, as if he thought Molly might be standing there. "I'm her father. Just give me the room number, I'll find it."

"Name?" she asked, working on her computer.

"Neil K-Y-D." She was busy typing and his impatience was boiling to the surface. He raised his voice. "Just tell me where she is?"

She looked over his shoulder for help. There was meant to be a security guard. She forced a smile. "May I see some ID?" She was stalling.

Kyd pulled out his new passport and handed it to her. She inspected it. "This isn't who you say you are."

Kyd realized it was Reynolds's passport. He didn't have time to argue a point he couldn't win. He reached in and turned the nurse's computer screen around so he could read it.

Stepping back, she yelled, "Security!"

Kyd found what he was looking for. He avoided the elevator and ran up the stairs. On the third floor, Kyd searched the room numbers until he came to 317 and pushed open the door.

Molly was lying in bed, her shaved head bandaged, dozing. She looked healthier, there was color in her cheeks. Margaret, seated, was startled to see a derelict, half-chewed—her son.

Kyd moved beside Molly's bed. "We've got to get out of here." He was looking to unplug her.

Margaret stood, in awe. "What happened to you?"

Kyd removed Molly's IV, and Margaret, aghast, pulled at his shoulder. "You can't do that."

Kyd slid his arms beneath his daughter and Margaret barked from behind. "Neil, stop!"

Molly woke up and smiled. "Daddy!" She had no trouble recognizing him.

"Hey, sweet pea, sorry to disturb your sleep, but we've got to go."

"I can walk." She was still in her green hospital gown.

He put her down, and she gingerly put her feet on the floor, using his hand to steady her. He led her to the door; she was careful.

"Are we going home?" Molly wanted to know.

"There's no place like home, right?" They were moving at glacial speed. He turned to Margaret. "Can you get her stuff?" Molly had proved she could walk. "Honey, can I carry you?" he asked, needing to pick up the pace.

She could feel his anxiety. "Okay." She put her arms around his neck as he lifted her. "Your breath smells funny," Molly noted.

"Coffee and hot dogs."

Margaret watched, increasingly disturbed. Her son had become unhinged. "Neil, tell me what's going on."

"We don't have time now." He carried Molly out the door, while Margaret hastily collected Molly's clothes from the closet.

Margaret caught up with them at the elevator and stated what she thought was obvious. "She needs to finish her treatment."

"She'll come back, but right now we need to be home where it's safe," Kyd insisted.

As they came out of the elevator on the ground floor, the security guard was waiting, speaking on his walkie-talkie. He stopped talking when he saw Kyd carrying Molly.

The nurse, still behind the counter, called out, "That's him! He can't take her, he has no ID."

Kyd spoke to Molly. "Tell them who I am."

Molly cleared her throat. "He's my father. We're going home."

Kyd skirted the guard, who was unsure what to do. Kyd tried to help. "If you want to shoot me, go ahead."

Margaret followed with Molly's clothes, shrugging at the bewildered guard as apology.

The nurse, in a last-ditch effort, yelled after Kyd, "The doctor hasn't checked her out! You need to be checked out!"

Kyd drove, bent over the steering wheel, concentrating on the winding road ahead. It was familiar, but tricky, with icy turns. There was no sign of a snowplow, and he didn't have tire chains. Heavy flakes floated in the headlights.

Margaret cradled her granddaughter in the back. "When will you tell me what we're doing?"

Kyd noted that "we're" included her in whatever crazy escapade her son had cooked up. Margaret, like Kyd, saw family as an unbreakable bond. How else could they have tolerated his old man for so many years? His bullying? Sometimes, it seemed to Kyd, she was still trying to make up for his crappy childhood. When Kyd had gotten older, she confided, "If I had to do it all over again, I wouldn't marry your father." She would momentarily forget that Kyd and Molly were products of their union. It was only after the old man died that she'd emerged from her shell. She loved Patty and Molly even more. Margaret could be iron-willed when it came to protecting her granddaughter. Kyd loved her for that.

Margaret's voice was no more than a constant buzz from the back seat, but she didn't give up, speaking in a loud whisper Molly could easily hear. "She hasn't finished her treatment," Margaret repeated. "Do you even know what you're doing?"

Kyd looked in the mirror to see his mother's concerned face and conceded. "I'm trying to keep you safe. I know how these people operate and we're better off at home where I can protect you."

"What people, Neil? What are you talking about?" She asked the question as if they were discussing a poltergeist.

Kyd retreated into his head, planning, too distracted to explain.

.

By the time Wexler reached Wichita, the sky had darkened. Thick, dark clouds were rolling in. Wexler entered the clinic with two male agents dressed for hunting, both wearing parkas. The nurse, at reception, recognized Wexler immediately, but didn't know his official status until he showed her his ID. She couldn't return his friendly smile, she was still traumatized.

"I wonder if you've seen this man?" Wexler showed her Kyd's passport photo.

She hardly needed a glance. "He took his daughter without permission. Her treatment wasn't over."

"Did he say where he was taking her?" Wexler asked.

"Home," she replied.

"When did they leave?"

She checked her watch. "Maybe forty minutes ago."

Wexler didn't bother to thank her, he left quickly with the two other agents following close behind.

The nurse's words followed him out. "She wasn't checked out!"

47

KYD'S HEADLIGHTS ILLUMINATED their farmhouse, the virgin snow a bright reflection. Kyd parked close to the house, noticing the tractor was gone and the hole for the septic tank had been covered with a black tarp.

He couldn't help but ask. "What happened to the tractor?"

"Todd, from next door, got it going and put it in the barn. He knew what he was doing."

Kyd couldn't be bothered replying to his mother's thinly veiled insult. He stuffed the video disk in his pocket, got out of the car, and opened Molly's door. "Can I carry you inside?" She easily folded into him.

They entered the house, Kyd and Molly, then Margaret with Molly's clothes. Kyd was comforted to see nothing had changed, the Earth still revolved around the Sun. Kyd settled Molly on the couch, tucking a blanket around her. "You okay here? Need oxygen or anything?"

Molly looked up at him, her eyes clear, speaking like a veteran of foreign wars. "Just tell us what to do." She wasn't frightened of anything.

"Can you light a fire?" Margaret asked.

Kyd replied on his way to the kitchen. "We're not staying."

"Where are we going? We only just arrived." Without his reply, his mother followed her son into the kitchen. She watched from the doorway.

Kyd hurriedly filled a tin bucket with supplies he found on the shelves, in the cupboard and drawers—canned goods, a can opener and a knife. He seemed unsure if what he was throwing in was enough, or the right necessities, looking around for anything he might have overlooked. He then began filling a plastic container he'd found under the sink with water.

"You need to tell me what you're doing. You're acting like a crazy person," Margaret insisted, standing next to him. "Are you sure you're thinking straight?" Kyd had tuned her out, concentrating on finishing with the water. Margaret wasn't satisfied, unhappy about being ignored. "If you think we're in danger, why don't you call the police?"

Kyd turned off the water. "They can't help." He screwed on the lid to the container, once again surveying the kitchen, his eyes snagged by his mother's steely gaze. "These people are merciless, anything's possible." Kyd knew his mother must think he'd gone mad, but he couldn't help it. He took a step toward his mother and put his hands on her shoulders. "I know you can't understand, but you have to trust me. We can't waste time."

Margaret looked at the supplies Kyd had gathered. "It looks like you're expecting a tornado."

"Exactly like that," he told her.

Most farmers living in Tornado Alley, like the Kyds, had a shelter under the house. Theirs was under the kitchen, with the entrance outside. Even if the house was flattened, the occupants beneath could survive. Kyd's father would never let Kyd play in the shelter, he said it was for emergencies only. Kyd only found out later it was where his old man went to smoke and look through secretly stored boating magazines.

Kyd folded back the two iron doors, while Molly and Margaret, dressed in winter coats, stood behind him. Margaret had the bucket with supplies, while Kyd carried Molly's oxygen tank and the container with water. There was an air vent beside the doors.

"Everyone inside," Kyd directed.

Molly followed her grandmother down the steps, Margaret turning on the light. Kyd had a quick look into the darkness outside the house and saw nothing that shouldn't be there. He knew it was just a matter of time.

Inside the shelter, there was a discarded couch, a couple of folding chairs and a card table with a half-finished thousand-piece jigsaw puzzle. During the last tornado warning, the all clear was given before they had a chance to finish it. Kyd remembered the corner pieces were laid by Patty.

Margaret set down the supplies. "How long do you expect us to stay down here?"

"Until it's safe to come up," was the only answer he knew.

Molly sat on the couch and Kyd organized the oxygen tank next to her. He pointed to the bucket with supplies. "This should be enough to keep you going."

Molly took a breath from the oxygen tank. "What are you going to do?"

Kyd moved to where she was sitting and squatted down so that their faces were at the same level. "There are some people that want something I have, but if I give it to them, it'll make things worse." He glanced at Margaret before continuing. "I need you and Margaret to stay down here. Can you promise to do that for me?"

Molly swallowed hard, then nodded. Kyd stood and turned to Margaret. He pulled the small white envelope out of his pocket and held it out to her. "If anyone does get down here, this is what they'll want. Give it to them."

Margaret took the envelope. "This?" She weighed the small parcel in her hand, the way Zarefsky had. It seemed too small to cause so much trouble.

"Don't come up unless I tell you to. Are we clear on that?" There wasn't a clear reply, but no one objected. He walked to the bottom of the steps.

"Neil ..." Margaret called out, and Kyd stopped to hear what she had to say. "I know you're a secret agent, I've known all along." Margaret felt better getting that off her chest.

Under other circumstances he might have laughed. "I guess I am. Lock the doors after me." He disappeared up the stairs, shutting the doors, and Margaret locked them. She turned back to Molly, still on the couch, and nodded agreement, something they both understood.

Kyd went through the house turning off the lights, then entered his office, guided by the beam of a flashlight. When he saw how the chairs were arranged, he was reminded it was the same room where Wexler proposed the whole thing. Kyd reached up and pulled his rifle down from the rack. He couldn't be sure it still worked, but was reminded of his father's admonition. "A workman never blames his tools."

His phone rang twice, and Kyd picked up, hearing the voice he expected. Kyd answered in Russian, "I'm here."

Wexler was on a cell phone in his car, parked down the road, fifty-odd yards away. He was in the front passenger seat, with an agent behind the wheel and one in the back. They saw a momentary flash of light through Kyd's office window.

"So you are. You must be tired, it's a hard trip coming back from the dead," Wexler said. There was bitter humor in his voice. "You shouldn't have taken Molly out of the clinic, the treatments were working."

Kyd had to admit, "She does look better."

"There was a pause, before Wexler continued. "No one has to get hurt, Kyd. You're not a violent person. What does this little disk mean to you, anyway? Is it worth risking your life?"

"I think you've already made that choice for me," Kyd replied.

While Wexler spoke, the agents with him checked their assault rifles. He continued speaking in a reasonable tone. "If you give me the disk, you can go back to doing what you do. After all, wasn't that your mission all along?"

Using his flashlight, Kyd opened a drawer and found the box of rifle cartridges; they rolled around inside. When he poured out the box only two bullets landed on the desk. Kyd had the phone squeezed between his shoulder and ear. "It's been destroyed. I don't even know why you're here. It's a wasted trip on taxpayers' money." Kyd switched off his flashlight and opened the window. The sting of the stiff, sharp breeze brushed his face. It helped him concentrate. He saw the car's dome light come on. Kyd could make out three people, but he couldn't tell which one was Wexler. He knew in his gut they wouldn't let up. There was no real negotiation or compromise; that much he'd learned.

"Major Zarefsky told us differently." Wexler turned and yelled at the agent in the back. "Turn off the fucking light!"

The windshield exploded and the agent in the driver's seat slumped over the wheel.

Beneath the house, Margaret and Molly heard the shot. Molly lifted her oxygen mask. "Was that a gun?"

Margaret was sitting beside her on the couch, and said with false confidence, "Your dad knows what he's doing." She put her arm around her granddaughter, as much to comfort herself as Molly. "Did I ever tell you about the time your father killed the biggest stag in the county?" She pulled Molly close, and said almost to herself, "He never hunted after that."

Kyd's rifle was still aimed outside the window, his breath visible. The light had gone out in Wexler's car. Kyd put the last cartridge in his rifle, hoping it had the magic to kill at least one more of the invaders.

Wexler took the assault rifle from the dead agent and got out of the car. He directed the other agent with hand gestures. They would attack the house from opposite sides. Wexler was still on his phone as he moved through the shadows toward the house. "Still there? Let's work something out. Molly will continue to get her treatment and I'll get you off the hook for killing a US federal agent." Wexler scurried, crouched. He could see the other agent moving around the side of the house.

Kyd, rifle in hand, moved out of the office, through the hallway, living room, kitchen, then out the back door. He made his way around the house, careful to avoid the tarp-covered hole. Using his rental car for cover, he caught glimpses of Wexler and the other agent moving forward. He only had one bullet left and chose Wexler as the worthy recipient. Didn't they say familiarity breeds contempt? Wexler wasn't as agile as the other man, no doubt hindered by his cashmere coat and age, but he was moving in and out of the light. Kyd rested the barrel of his rifle on the hood of the car to steady his hand. Wexler paused; Kyd took a deep breath and fired. The bullet pinged off the detached backhoe. Kyd slid down behind the car. Given time, he knew Wexler would find the shelter. He had to lead them away from the house. Kyd sprinted toward the barn.

•

Margaret and Molly heard footsteps above, walking over the iron doors. Molly asked Margaret, "Is that Dad?"

Her voice was magnified through the air vent, and the agent, hearing this, stopped. Looking down, he saw the thin crack of light between the cellar doors.

Molly's voice came through the vent. "Dad?"

Molly and Margaret could hear someone tugging at the handles, then the muffled sound of the tractor's engine.

The agent, after a moment's indecision, gave up on the cellar and ran for the barn.

Wexler was holding Kyd's discarded rifle when the sound of the tractor's deep-throated growl got his attention. He had underestimated Kyd before, but not again. If Kyd were unreasonable, his family could be used as leverage. One way or another, he would get what he wanted.

With the doors closed and the barn completely in the dark, Kyd crouched under the tractor. The warmth of the engine didn't give him as much comfort as he'd hoped, but he had to admit, Todd, the neighbor-farmer, knew what he was doing. Kyd found a curved sickle hanging on the wall and waited. Kyd felt, with darkness as an aid, he might have a chance to slash one of the attackers when they came close enough to investigate.

■

Molly and Margaret stood at the foot of the stairs, Molly having left her oxygen tank behind. They could still hear the tractor's engine.

Molly spoke in a gasp, "He needs our help."

Margaret looked at Molly, considering, then back to the envelope resting at the center of the puzzle. "If that's what they want, they can have it." Margaret grabbed the envelope, then climbed the stairs.

·

Kyd, resting on the balls of his feet, held the handle of the sickle tight, waiting for his opportunity. He saw Wexler's silhouette coming through the entrance, the barrel of his assault rifle searching for a target.

Wexler spoke loudly, above the engine's noise. "You're in a hopeless position, you know that, don't you? Time to give up. My offer still stands. Do it for Molly."

Kyd had a hard time keeping track of Wexler as he moved in and out of the deepest shadows. His voice was closer, no more than a few yards away. "Shit, we'll die of carbon monoxide poisoning."

Kyd then saw the other agent coming through the back door, his eyes still not accustomed to the dark. Both stealthy figures moved toward the tractor.

In that moment, the engine stopped, out of fuel. There was a ballooning silence, and Kyd took a chance. "Here!" he shouted.

There was a burst of machine-gun fire from both agents, and one went down. Wexler, hoping he'd hit Kyd, moved past the tractor, and found the other agent lying on the barn's floor, unmoving, soaked in blood.

Kyd sprinted out, Wexler just having time to see his fleeing figure.

Molly and Margaret looked out of the living room window, seeing Kyd running toward the house. When Kyd saw them, he gestured angrily for them to get out of sight. Wexler, assault rifle in hand, was halfway behind Kyd.

Molly and Margaret ducked beneath the windowsill. Molly whispered to Margaret, "Dad wants him to fall into the hole."

Margaret peeked above the sill to see Wexler, and he spotted her before she could duck down again. He approached the front door, practically swaggering. "Let's not make this any tougher than it needs to be. Neither of us wants to put your family at risk." He knew Kyd could hear him.

Kyd watched Wexler from behind the back corner of the house. It had started to snow more heavily, flakes landing in his eyes. Kyd stepped out, so Wexler could see him. "Patty told me you asked her out once. She said you were sad. I don't think I saw it until now."

Wexler changed direction and walked toward Kyd. The tarped hole was between them. He pointed his rifle at Kyd's chest. "Where is it?"

Kyd took a step back. "If I had a dollar every time I was asked that ..."

Neither of them laughed. Wexler was at the edge of the hole. "I won't ask again." He prepared to fire when Margaret appeared behind Kyd.

"I've got it," Margaret said, holding up the envelope for Wexler to see.

Kyd turned, surprised and disappointed. "I told you to stay in the shelter."

"I'm not risking my granddaughter's life over this," Margaret replied. She stepped forward, beside Kyd, and spoke to Wexler. "Here, take it."

Wexler looked down at the tarp. "Bring it here and mind the hole."

Margaret stepped forward, sidestepping the tarp, when Kyd spotted Molly behind Wexler. She was quietly moving forward, building her strength.

Kyd pointed at Wexler's legs. "You've got a stain on your trousers."

Reflexively, Wexler looked down and Molly began running, shoving Wexler with all her might. He fell through the tarp and into the icy hole.

Wexler scrambled to get out, but the walls were too steep and slick with ice.

Molly, catching her breath, looked at her father. "We planned it," she said proudly.

"You promised to stay in the shelter," Kyd reminded her.

Wexler's voice came from the hole. "You shot a federal agent. I can help you."

Margaret reminded Kyd, "She saved your life."

Wexler interrupted again. "I helped Molly."

Kyd looked at Molly. "Go inside, it's cold out here." Then to Margaret he said, "Take her inside."

Margaret led Molly toward the house, but suspected Kyd's intentions. She stopped and turned toward him. "Remember, Neil, you're a decent human being and a father."

"I'll remember." Kyd watched them go inside.

Wexler yelled out, "I'll freeze in here."

"Throw out your gun," Kyd demanded.

Wexler's assault rifle landed at Kyd's feet, and Kyd looked down at Wexler. "Why? Why, Paul? What was this about?" He still couldn't balance what had happened against the rewards.

Wexler's voice echoed up without much conviction. "You know why. Garin heard about the disk and was worried Nicoli would win."

"Because you told them about it," Kyd reminded him. "You set me up to be killed."

Wexler began to dance, his feet jogging in place. "Don't pretend you don't know what we do. All's fair in love and war, right?" Wexler saw Kyd's head over the hole. He couldn't read his expression. "I can't feel my feet."

"Irina was tortured to death. I saw her body." Kyd expected Wexler to pretend remorse.

"That was going to happen anyway." Wexler looked up. "If you're going to kill me, get it over with." Wexler hadn't given up on Kyd's humanity. He knew Kyd was infected with morals.

"What did they give you to turn?" Kyd asked.

Wexler surprised Kyd with a dismissive laugh. "Turn? It's not black hats and white hats. It's all the same with different flags. It comes down to who pays the best—holiday houses, expensive restaurants, cars. It's a great get-out-of-jail-free card."

It was true; Wexler wasn't telling him anything he didn't already know. They were things he'd tried not to see. Kyd climbed the ladder next to the water tank. "I won't kill you, Paul."

Wexler saw Kyd at the top of the ladder and knew he was in for some kind of payback, without knowing what that might be. His voice betrayed his growing panic. "I can get Molly back into the program. You can't say I didn't do what I promised."

Kyd looked to the sky then down at Wexler. "The sky's clearing. Can you see the stars? It'll get colder. We farmers are always concerned with the weather."

Wexler was begging. "Tell me what I can do. What can I do to make this right? You tell me. There's plenty of money."

Kyd had his hand on a lever beneath the tank. "There's a heating coil that keeps the water from freezing. You'll feel warm for a minute."

Wexler hadn't given up hope. "This makes no sense. What will you get out of it?"

"You'll know soon." Kyd pulled the lever and the water gushed out, soaking Wexler, his cashmere overcoat looking like the skin of a sea otter. Kyd looked down at Wexler's pathetic figure and turned off the water. "Quid pro quo, isn't that the phrase you used, Paul? You did something for me, now I'm doing something for you." Anger was creeping into his voice, he couldn't hold it back. "Try to imagine what it was like for Irina. Hanging naked, beaten and gouged. Treated like a piece of meat. Picture that. You're getting off easy."

Wexler took off his gloves, clawing at the slick walls, desperately hoping to find a hold, but it was useless.

Kyd's face disappeared from view as Wexler pleaded, "Kyd! ... Kyd! ... Keep the fucking disk, it's yours! You can do what you want with it!"

48

THE SKY WAS brightening, and as Kyd predicted, there had been a cold bump, or at least that's what the weatherman called it. Paramedics had rescued Wexler's body from the hole. He couldn't move his arms or legs, his face was blue, and his coat was a stiff sheet of ice. He was alive, but frostbite would most likely claim the tips of his fingers, toes, ears and nose. Was it enough?

There were two ambulances, a coroner's van, and a couple of unmarked government sedans in front of the house. Kyd had called it in and the response was quick, much quicker than he got in Russia. He hadn't explained much more than the thin results. They'd figure out the rest. He was watching his government do the cleanup as he drank from a steaming mug of coffee. Paramedics carried two black bags with the dead agents to the van. They probably had families that would wonder what happened to them. The Agency would say they'd died with honor.

Barnes, in what looked like a new down parka and wool beanie, came out of the house and approached Kyd. She looked uncomfortably preserved, the prototype for a "real" person.

She surprised him with sarcasm. "Quite a party," she said.

A new black sedan approached, using a path that was becoming well-worn. It parked on the other side of the coroner's van.

"He'll want to talk to you," Barnes said.

Kyd didn't know who this newest arrival could be, but given the quickness that Barnes walked to the car, they had to be higher up the food chain. When she got to the car, the back window slid down. Barnes had a brief conversation with the rider then waved Kyd over. It was time to deal.

She opened the back door, inviting Kyd to enter, and he threw out what was left of his coffee, handing Barnes the empty mug. Once inside, Barnes shut the door.

Sorrow told the driver, "We'll be okay, but leave the engine running, we need the heat." The driver got out, leaving the two men alone. Sorrow offered his hand to shake but Kyd couldn't be bothered.

"Clyde Sorrow," he said, and lowered his hand.

How would this go? Like most things in Kyd's life, it was impossible to predict. Despite what could be called "winning," Kyd wasn't satisfied, he never would be.

Sorrow said, "I saw you used to work in our language department. You did good work." When Kyd didn't respond, Sorrow continued, "Nice place you've got here, not too big, not too small."

Kyd could tell Sorrow wasn't like Wexler—he came across as practical, bureaucratic. There was nothing about him that stood out. This was the way spies were meant to look, anonymous.

Sorrow took a moment to assess Kyd, trying to see the man who had outwitted the Russians. Kyd didn't come across as James Bond and Sorrow smiled to himself. He could relate to men like Kyd.

The coroner's van drove away with its cargo.

Sorrow broke the silence. "Cold out here. I grew up in Nebraska, but this ..."

Kyd waited.

Sorrow rubbed his thighs. "Well, what a clusterfuck, eh?" He wanted confirmation from Kyd, but when there was none, he continued. "It was meant to be a simple operation. Now everyone's pissed off. The Russians, the president, even me. Poor Wexler's a human Popsicle, his beautiful clothes ruined." Sorrow smiled.

Kyd couldn't care less about Sorrow's problems. He was still looking for answers and knew Sorrow would eventually fill the void.

"If you had the disk, it would help. It would mean something," Sorrow let him know.

"This was your operation?" Kyd asked, his voice flat. His breath fogging the side window.

"We, the government of the United States of America, reached an agreement with the Russian president." Sorrow sighed. "If we could help him defeat Petrov, we'd get assistance with Iran and some oil interests. Our part of the deal was to deliver the video disk so Petrov couldn't use it, and they didn't want to be embarrassed internationally." Sorrow wanted Kyd to understand. He had no trouble feeling Kyd's resentment. "Petrov's sister is the one who got you involved."

Kyd turned to look at him. "And I was the sacrificial lamb, is that it?"

"How can I put it? The assassination was a bit impromptu. I suppose you being there was too big an opportunity for them to pass up, American spy and all." Sorrow paused. "Of course, Paul let us down, not as loyal as we would have liked."

"You could have pulled us out," Kyd said.

"We needed the disk to make things work." Then he remarked as if awarding a bronze medal, "If it's any consolation, all of us on this side are glad you got out."

"Nicoli and Irina weren't so lucky." The images came back to him.

Sorrow wasn't good with sympathy, he still saw operations as a board game with bloodless pieces. "There's still a chance this could be worth what everyone sacrificed. Their deaths wouldn't be in vain." Sorrow had a hard time giving the impression that he cared. "Do you have the disk, Neil?" No one called him Neil but his mother.

Kyd didn't really know what he would do next, it was an unconscious thing, but he surprised Sorrow by leaning over him and locking his door. Sorrow was even more surprised when Kyd landed the first punch, breaking his nose. Kyd couldn't stop, even when Sorrow was flat on the seat. Kyd wanted him to feel what he felt.

It took Barnes a moment to register what was happening. She and the driver tried Sorrow's door. Then the driver pulled Kyd out the other side. Sorrow was conscious, moaning, his face was flattened and bloody.

Once out of the car, and restrained by the agents who had rushed over, Kyd saw Molly watching from the living room window. He turned away.

49

THREE WEEKS LATER, Molly, with short punk hair she'd dyed purple, was back in the clinic sitting up in bed. Kyd, clean-shaven with laundered clothes, stood beside her. He'd only had limited communication with the Agency but knew that was about to change. They were getting their ducks in a row. Garin, with no serious opposition, had been reelected in a landslide, no longer needing American help. The investigation into Nicoli Petrov's assassination ended when Irina Petrov, wracked with guilt, committed suicide soon after her co-conspirator, Douglas Reynolds, did the same.

Margaret was seated in the chair she'd claimed earlier.

"I think they're almost ready to throw you out," Kyd said to Molly.

Molly smiled. "They only want to see how everything's working." She looked at him as though she could see into his brain. "Are you okay?"

"No complaints."

"Neil?" Margaret pointed at Agent Barnes standing in the doorway, carrying a briefcase.

He walked out to meet her in the corridor.

"How's Molly doing?" Barnes asked. She seemed genuinely interested but it was hard to tell.

"You have something for me?" Kyd asked, cutting to the chase.

"There's always paperwork. You want to go somewhere?" she asked, uncomfortable being in the public corridor.

"No reason to hide, right?" Kyd replied, knowing they were professional hiders.

She opened her briefcase and took out a document. "We need you to sign this in a few places." She handed him the paperwork. Yellow tabs were sticking out, flagging the places needing signatures. "This guarantees Molly's continued treatment through the end of the program. We'll pay for everything, and I can tell you, these treatments aren't cheap."

"I pay taxes." Kyd leafed through the agreement, full of promises written in wet sand.

"It also absolves you of any crimes you may have committed." She had a pen in her hand and Kyd took it. She lowered her voice. "In return, we get the video disk."

Kyd began signing. "What will you do with it?"

"Above my pay grade," she said, ducking the question. "Did you ever watch it?"

"Didn't need to." Kyd handed her the signed papers. He went into Molly's room, reached under the mattress and pulled out the little white envelope. Molly and Margaret watched him hand it to Barnes.

After she put it in her briefcase, she had one more thing to say. "I've been reminded to tell you that everything that happened in Russia and what came after is covered by the National Security Act."

Kyd surprised her by grabbing the lapel of her jacket, pushing her away from the door and against the wall. His face was close to hers. "And I want to make something crystal clear, I don't want anything happening to my family. They've got nothing to do with any of it. Understand?"

Barnes squirmed away, unsettled, trying to regain her composure. "You've got nothing to worry about." Barnes backed away further, unsure if Kyd would attack her again. She turned, click-clacking down the polished linoleum.

"Daddy?" Molly called from inside.

"I'm here." He reentered the room.

50

THE VIDEO BEGAN with the missile strikes. The chamber was silent. All the Security Council members' eyes were on the large screen over the podium. The young woman's camcorder captured the dog then the boy falling to the ground in convulsions. The tape was advanced. When the inspectors arrived and began speaking Russian, the Russian ambassador spoke up. "This is a trick, you can do anything with video. Where did this come from? What is the source?"

"You know this to be true," the US ambassador said, her voice rock steady. "There are no tricks. Russia was complicit."

The video finished and the lights grew bright. The US ambassador turned to her colleagues, all digesting what they'd seen, looking toward the Russian ambassador. "Does anyone still have doubts why Russia has used its Security Council veto eleven times to shield its allies in Damascus from condemnation, sanctions or referral to the International Criminal Court?" She glared at the Russian ambassador. "You asked me for proof, here is your proof."

"Ridiculous!" The Russian ambassador rose and walked out followed by his entourage.

51

THE TRACTOR WAS idling as Kyd attached the backhoe. He stopped to pour himself coffee from the thermos. There were only patches of snow left, slowly melting. He looked into the distance, watching a deer nibbling the new grass. He took a sip, steam rising, when the deer bolted.

His coffee cup exploded. Kyd staggered, then collapsed.

The shooter, dressed in white camouflage, disassembled her rifle, red hair falling to her shoulders.

Acknowledgements

I would first like to thank Cheryl Bailey, my life partner, who was willing to read early drafts and offer polite advice. I would also like to thank Chris Fitchett, my office mate, who took the time to give witty and relevant tips. To Ron Rosenberg, brother and critic, who liked an early draft and encouraged me to continue. And Chris Leach, new friend and serious reader, who despite preferring nonfiction, found *Kyd's Game* entertaining and caught several mistakes. I would be remiss if I didn't also acknowledge and wholeheartedly thank the Vine Leaves Press crew for their encouragement and support. Jessica Bell kindly accepted my submission, Amie McCracken did a fine job editing, and Peter Snell was the first serious and enthusiastic reader.

I would also like to plug Bill Browder's *Red Notice*, a nonfiction book that reads like a novel, once more drawing attention to the brutality of the Russian government. This was certainly one of my inspirations for *Kyd's Game*. The war in Ukraine is further evidence of Vladimir Putin's cruel megalomania.

Vine Leaves Press

Enjoyed this book?
Go to *vineleavespress.com* to find more.
Subscribe to our newsletter:

Printed in Australia
Ingram Content Group Australia Pty Ltd
AUHW020633031024
400715AU00012B/80